AF290950

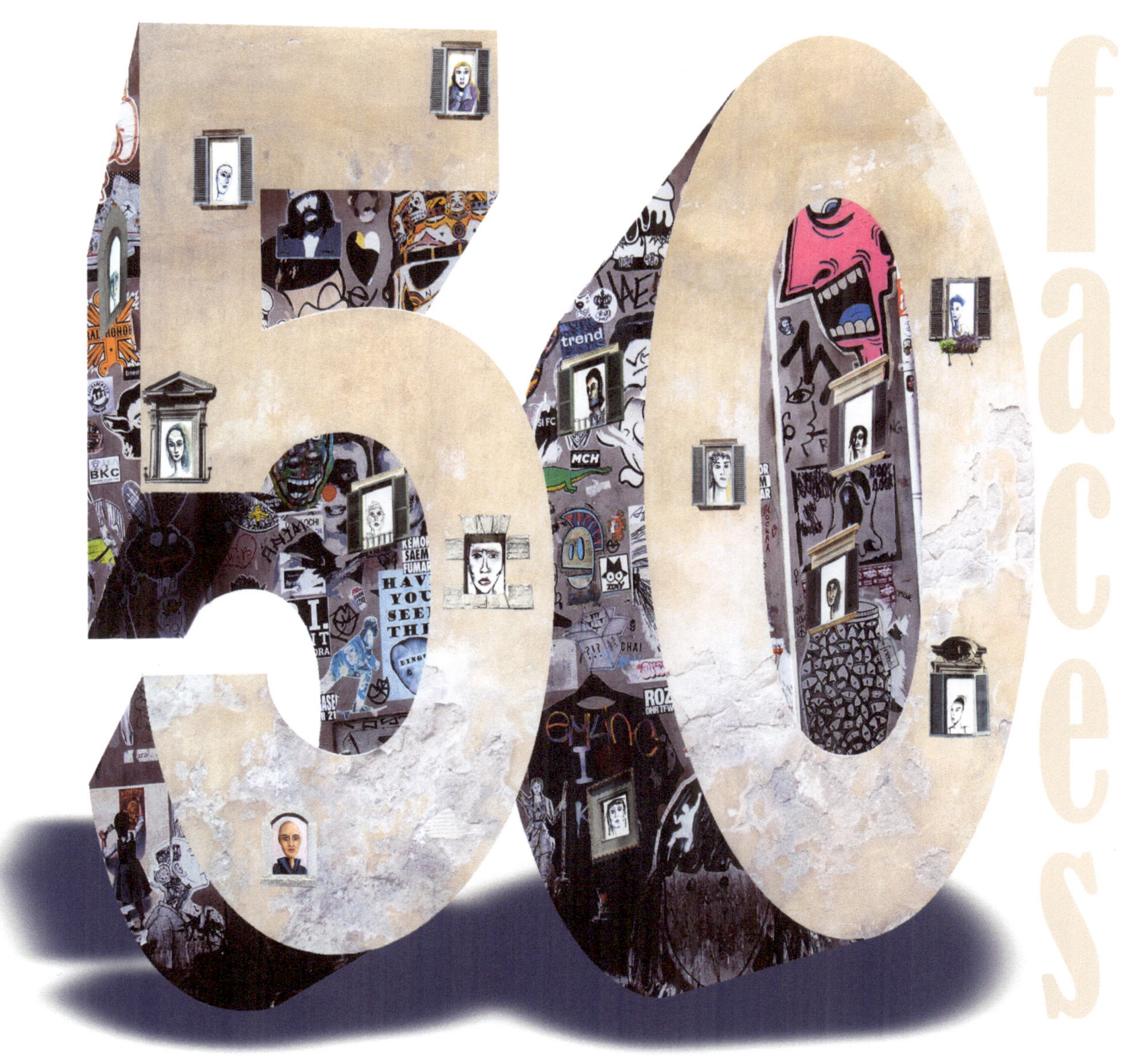

illustrated portrait art

Jill Robb

50 friends, family, colleagues, strangers, legends and any combination thereof, Welcome you to your new face gallery—yay! Time to make it your own.

This book has 50 faces, OK you got me, there are ~ 51, but each and every one is essential, and you paid for the extra page anyway, so do with them what you will.

These faces are a visual reminder that it is exactly what makes a face 'funny', that is the unique and beautiful thing that you love about someone. It is why we are all the different, and why we are all the same, Every face - everyone is precious, and we are all essential.

Ways to explore this book

Passive

Observer
Get to know the faces and really see them for what they are.

Contemplator
Get to know the faces and contemplate *who* they are— *What* do they have to say?
Do this over the years, and eventually end up getting frustrated that they haven't aged a day and throw this old book of young faces away (to charity- of course).

Interactively
Use the blank pages to make this book yours.

Storyteller/ tribe creator
Have some fun, create your own tribe and story up the pages.
What is their name? Where do they live? What do they do? What are their quarks? Write their story- if you get stuck, just wait and evolve it over time.
Write whatever comes to mind- just make sure you stay between the lines (Pst there are none#).

Doodler/Artist
Draw their life, is it in a window? In a picture frame, or the face of some mystical beast?

Self-experiment of how you perceive people
Write the date, and your thoughts of each face, whatever comes to mind. Repeat this exercise over time, each time not reading what you have previously written until after you have added your new entry.
Have your thoughts about them changed? Were your thoughts more to do with where you were at that moment? What *you* were doing? Your aims? Does your mood affect your judgment?

Your Special idea
Go on— I know you want to, you're thinking it right now, this book would be perfect for it, I agree, I think you should do it, it's your book, do what you like with it, if you ever feel you have ruined it, you can always cut the page out or - buy another book :)

Have fun with your 50 new faces, they will be here for you whenever you need them, and remember– the most beautiful face is one that is truly smiling.

(#there are currently none, but if they help you write- rule away!

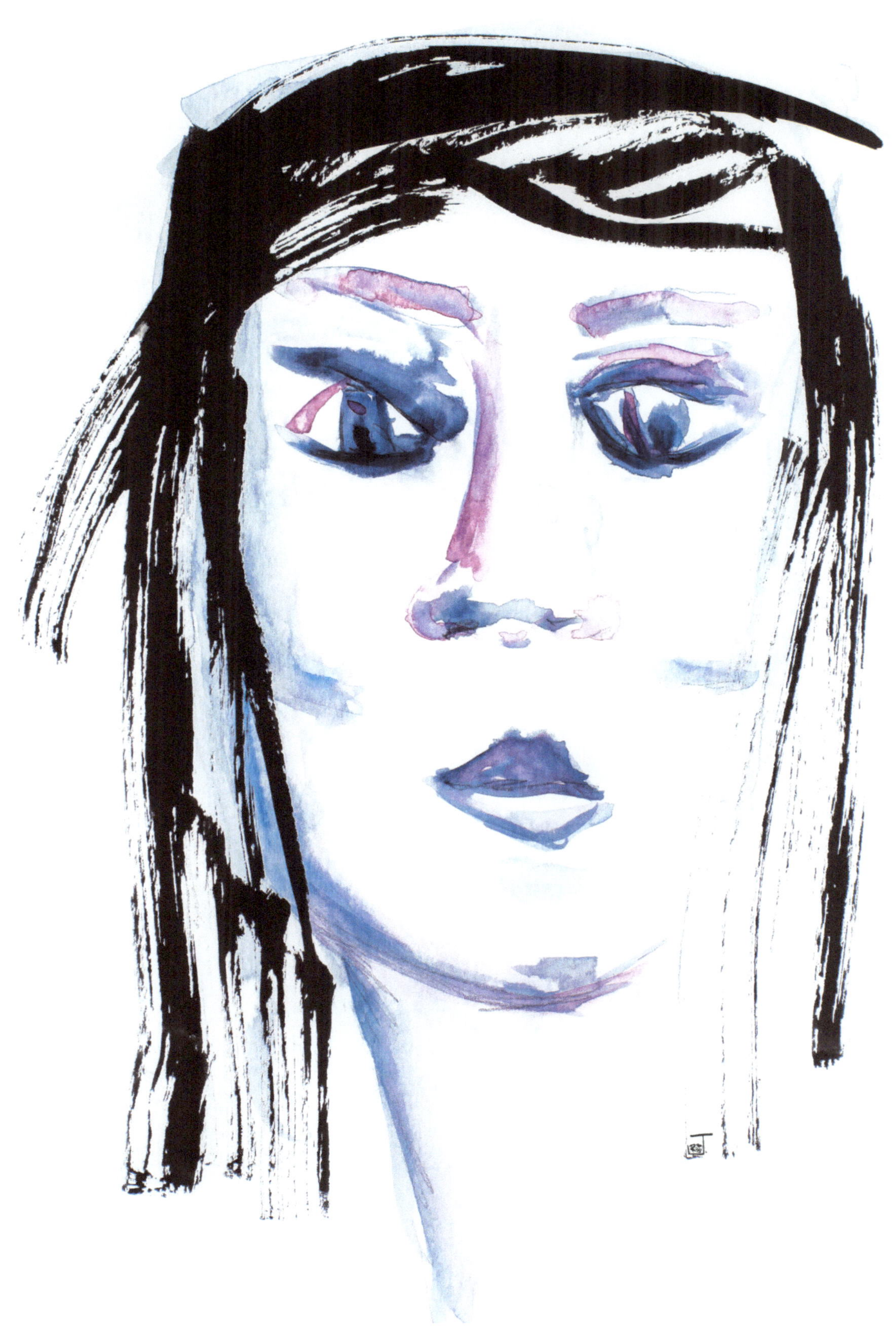

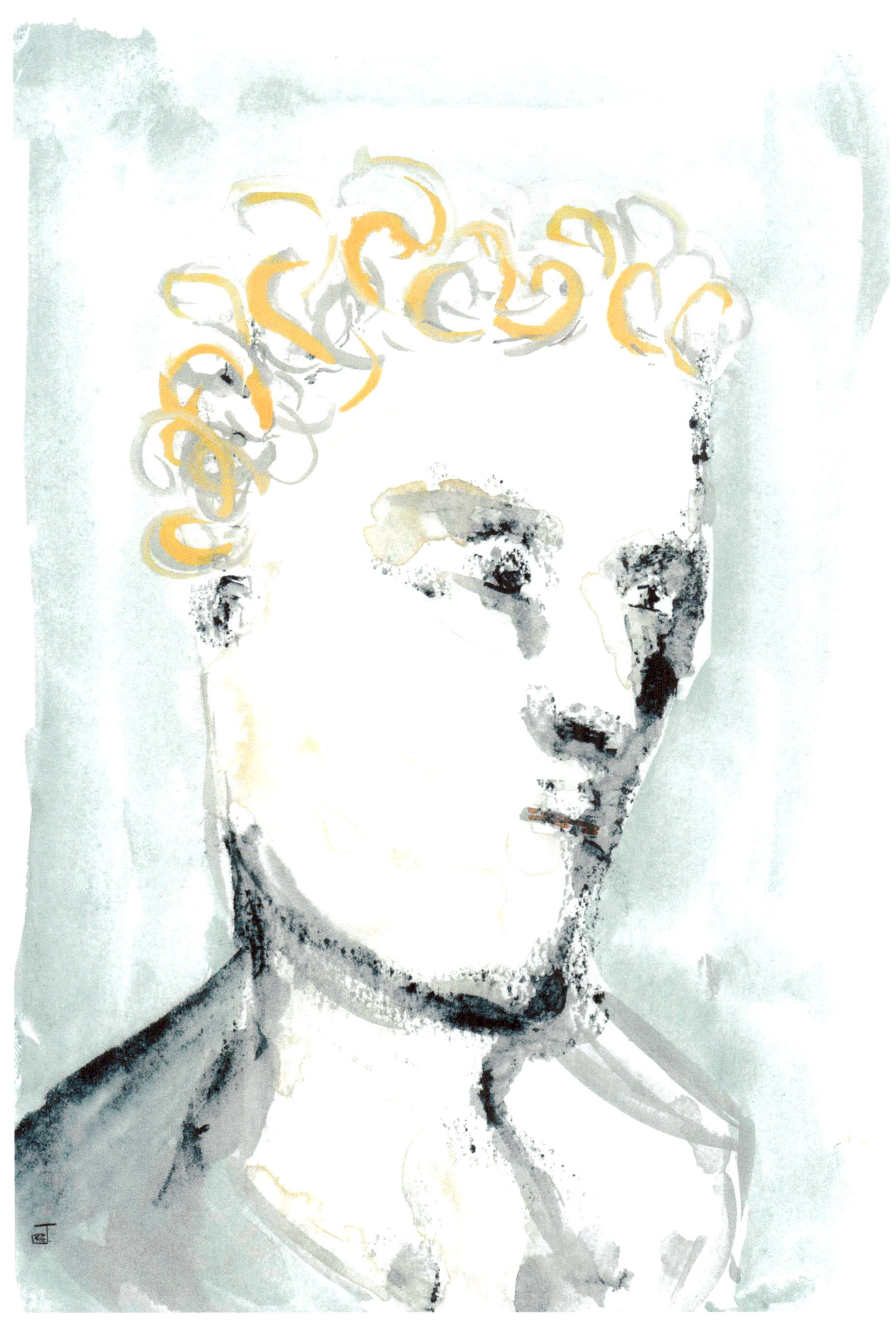

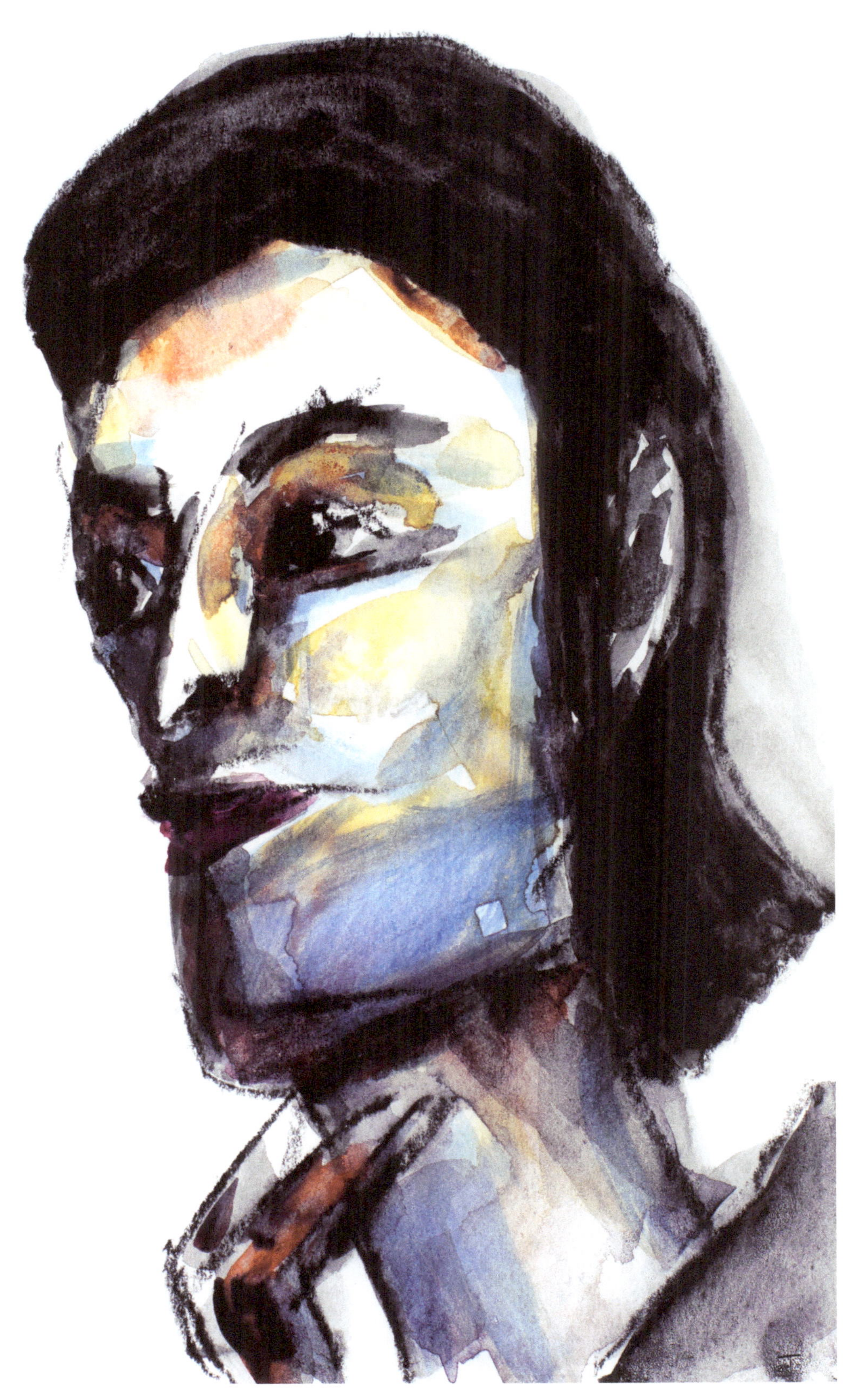

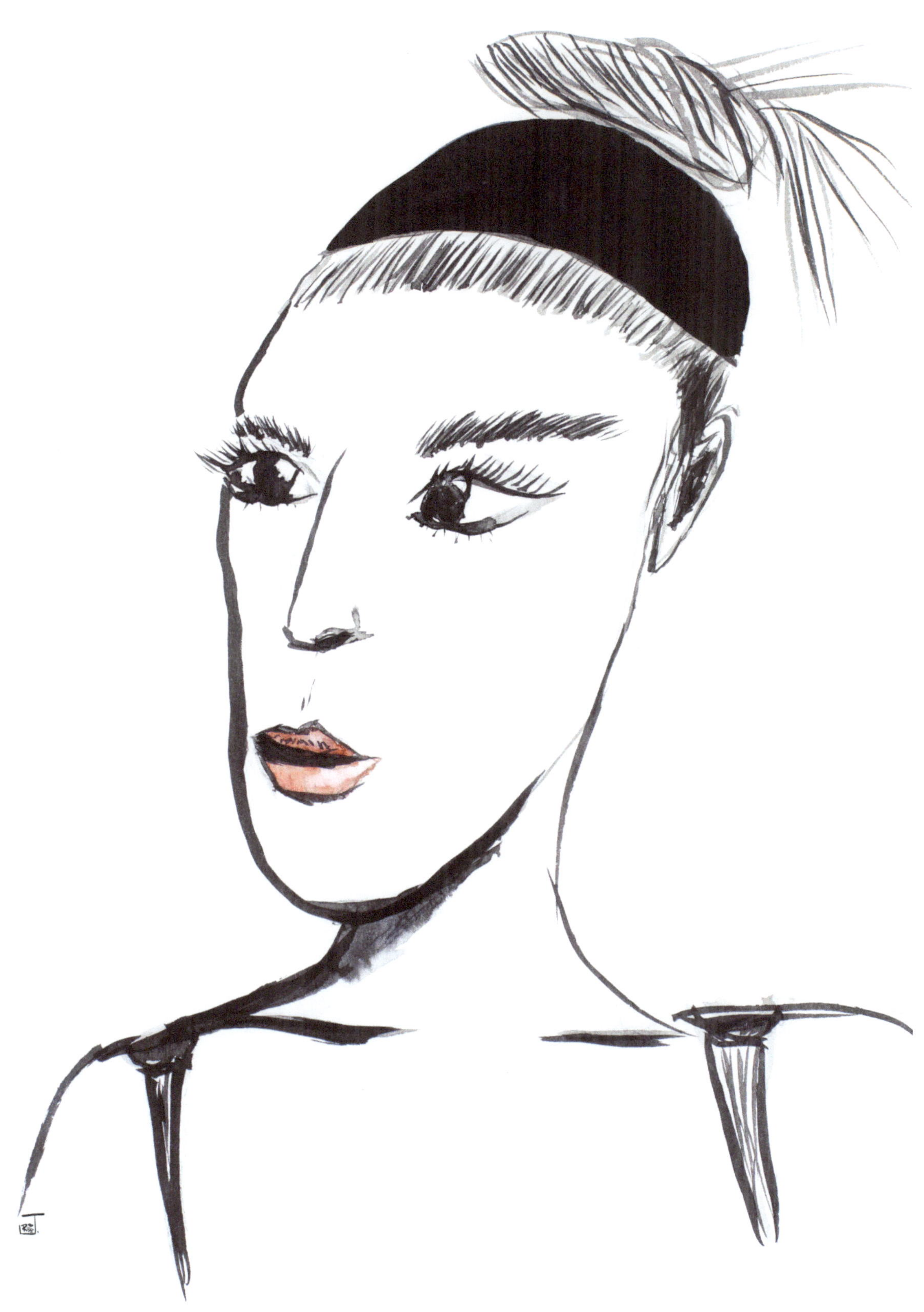

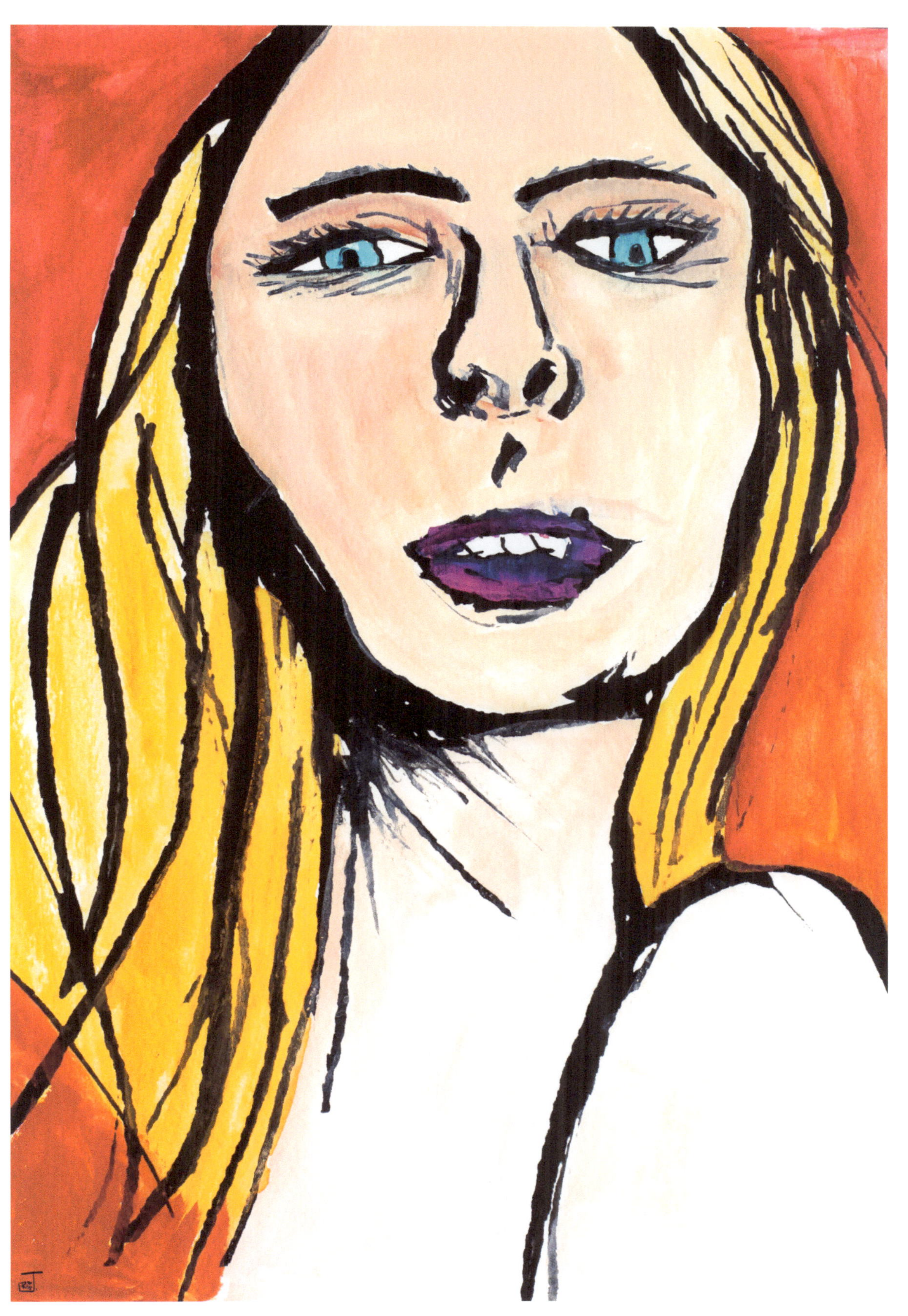

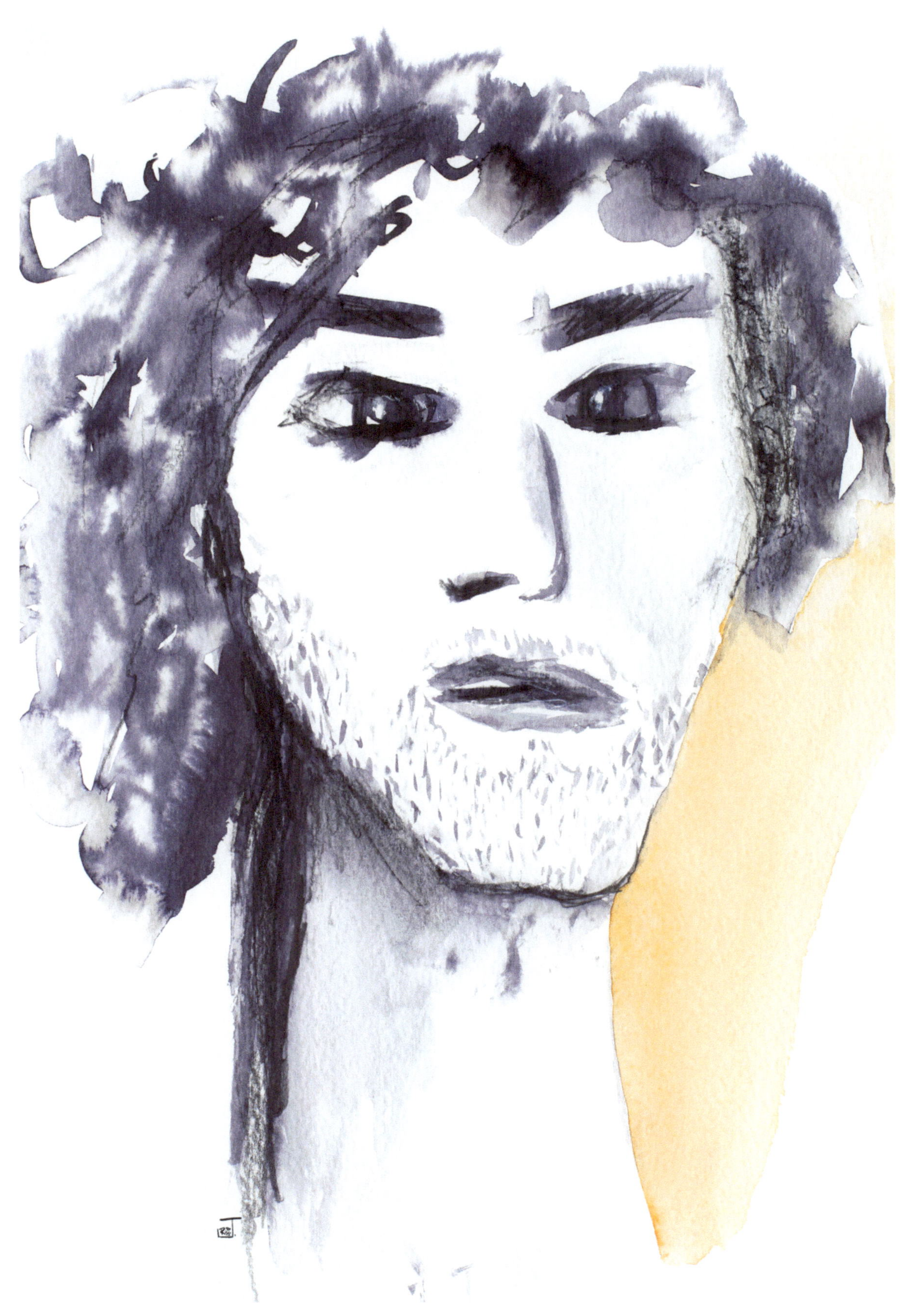

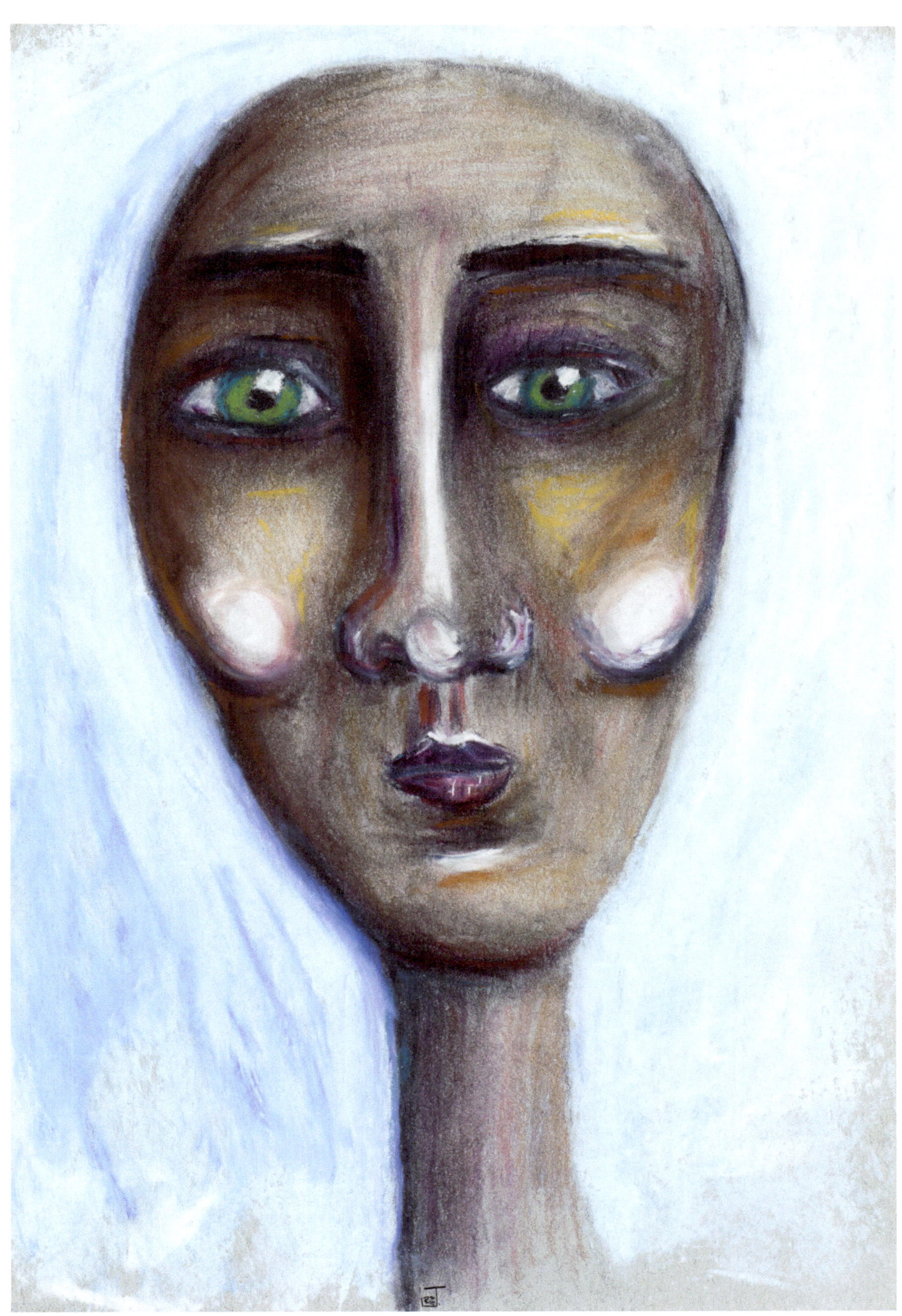

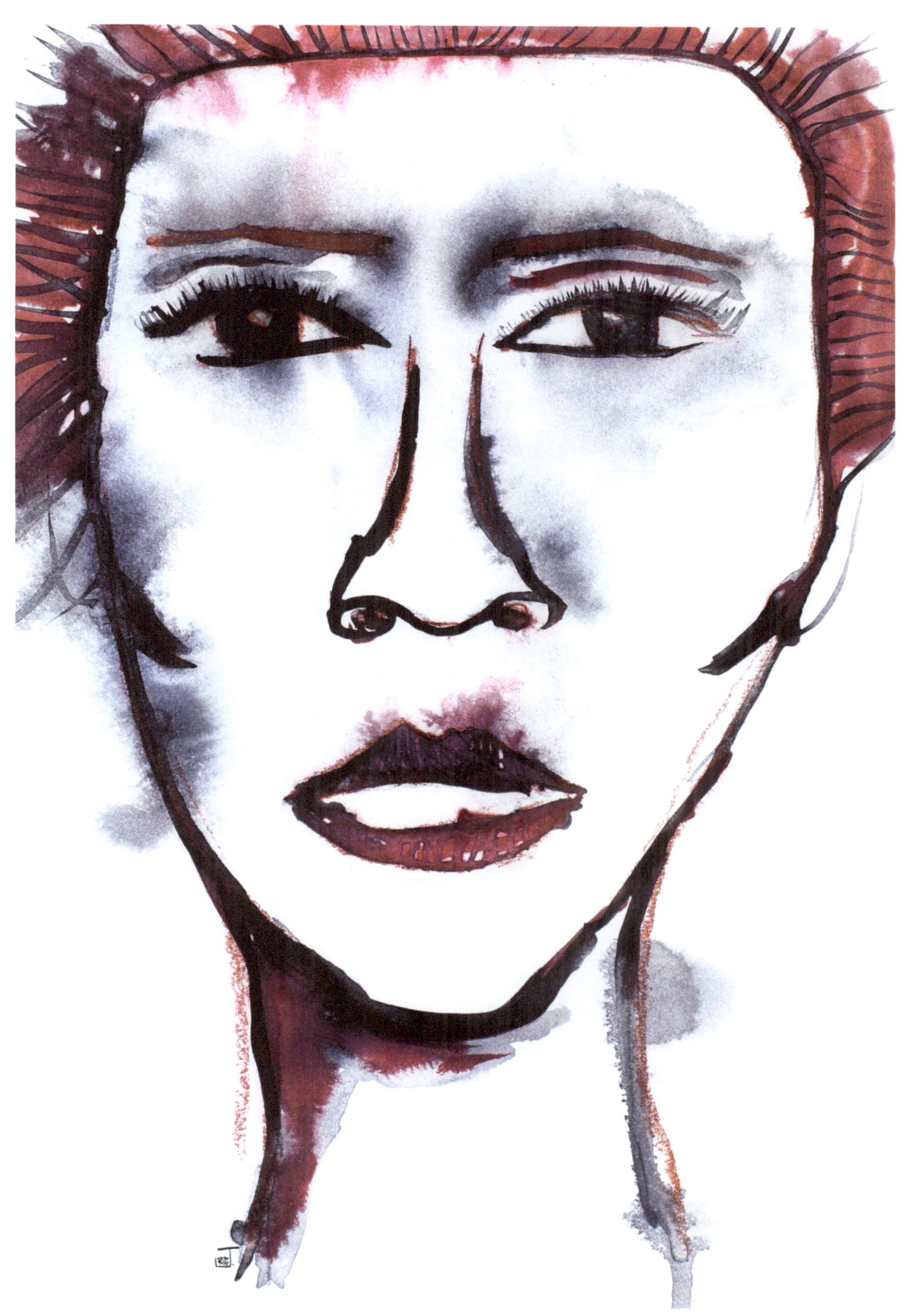

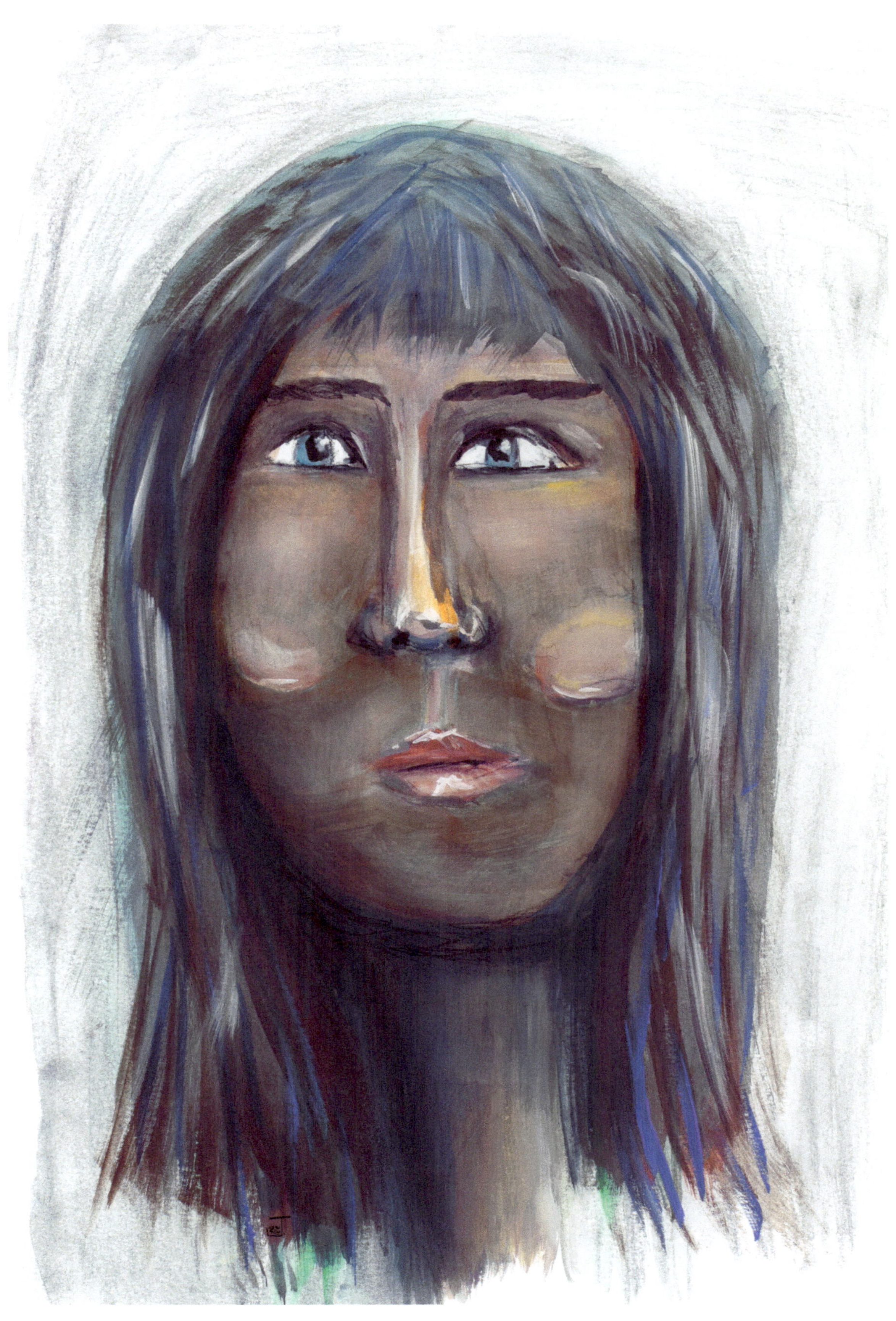

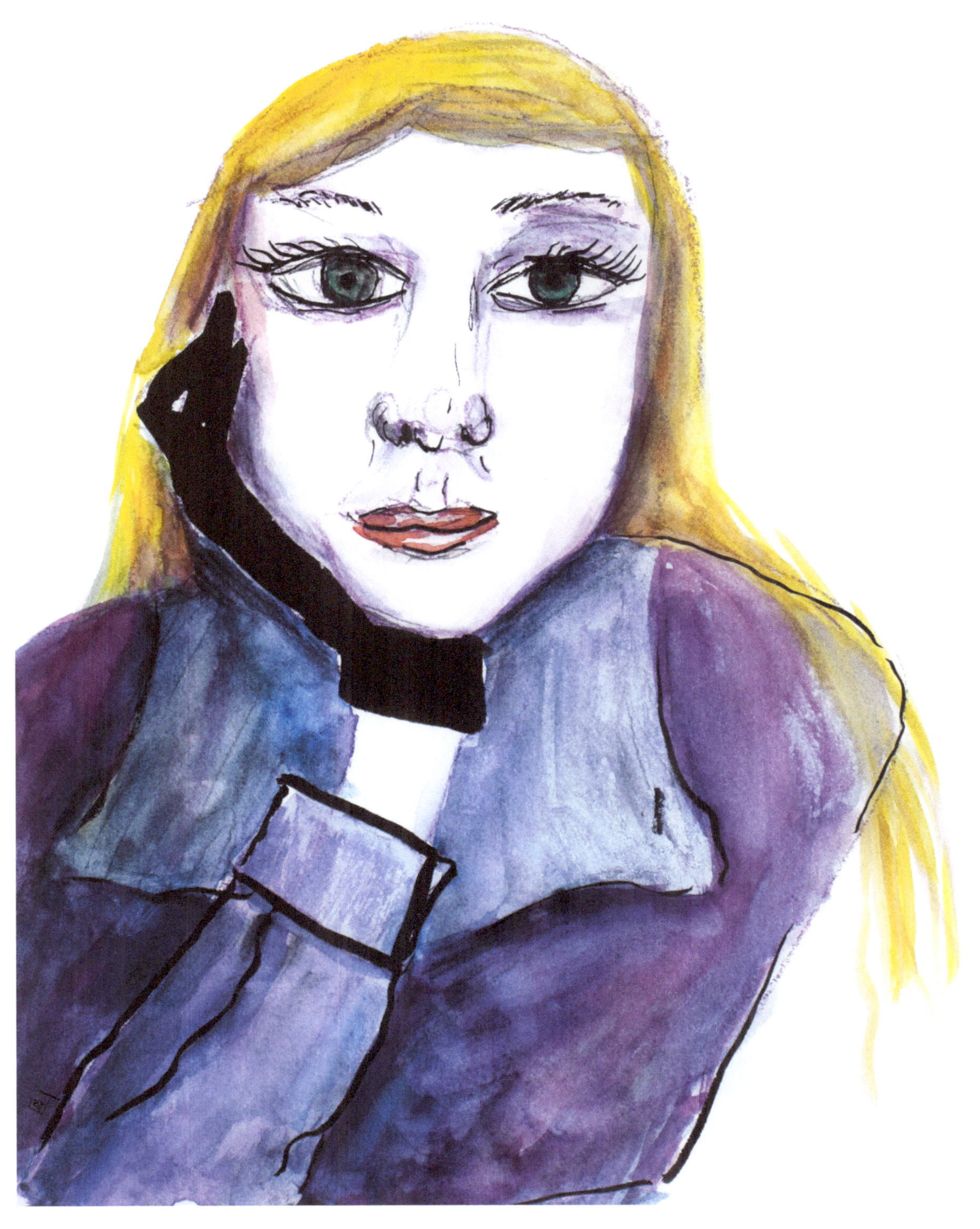

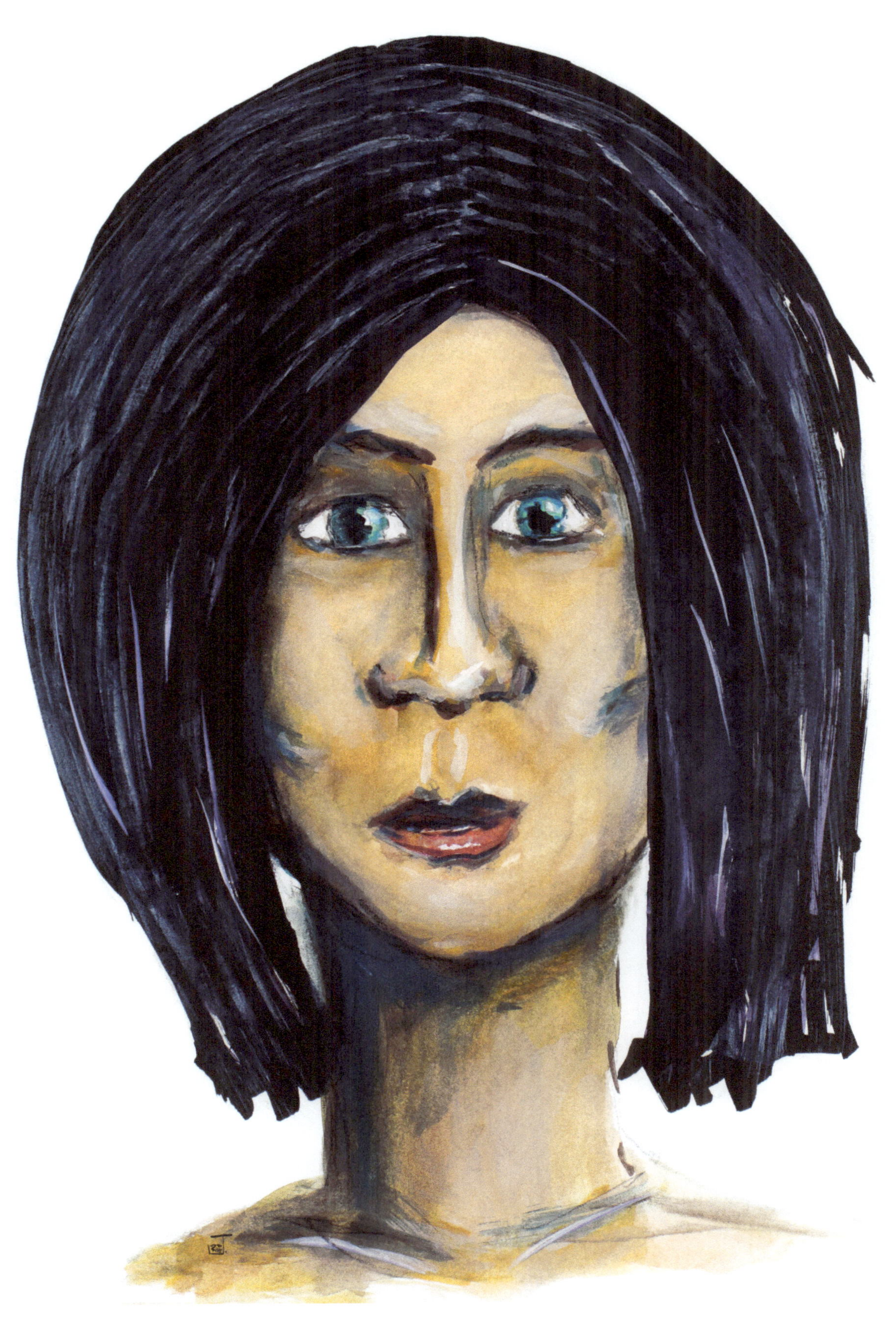

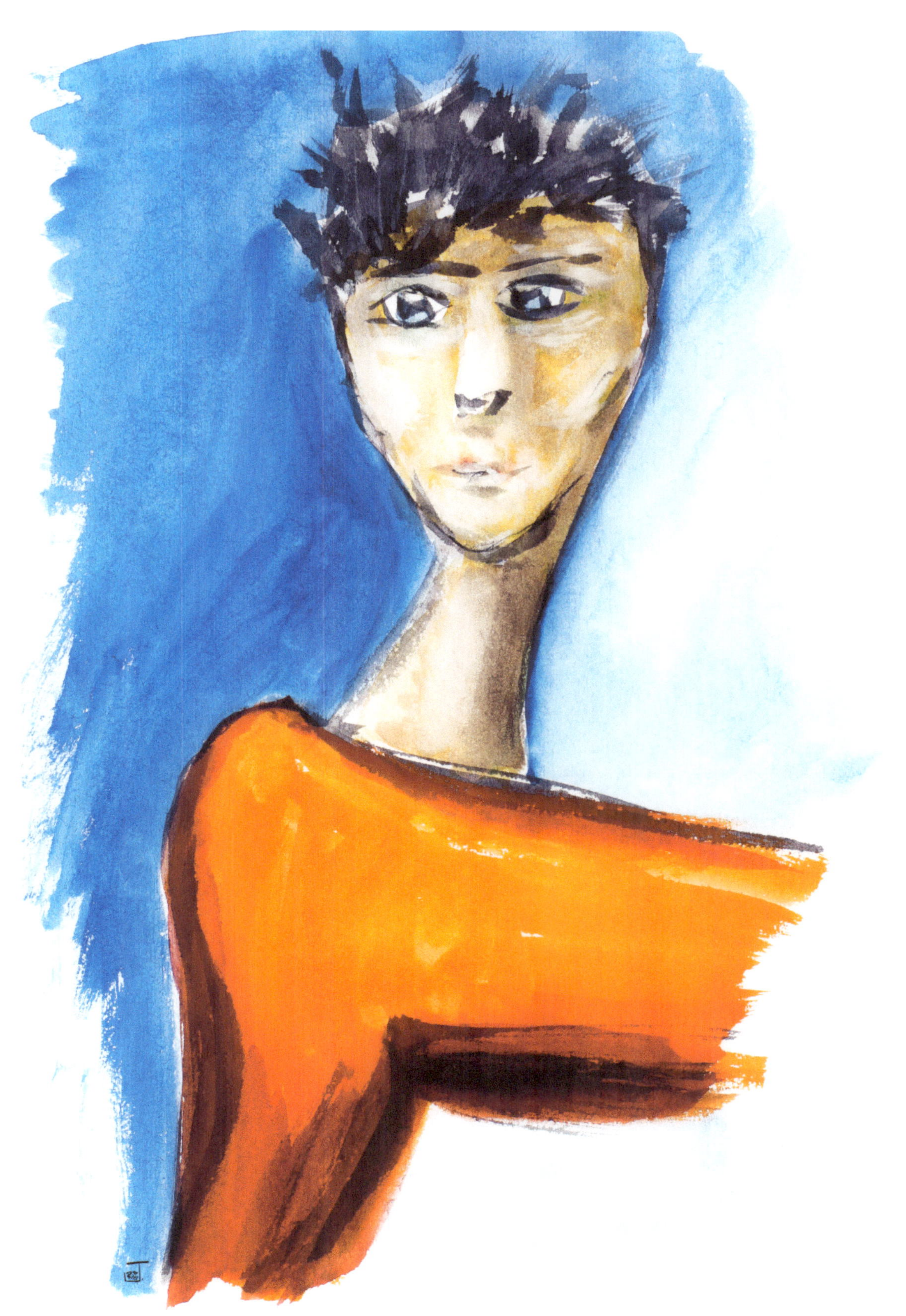

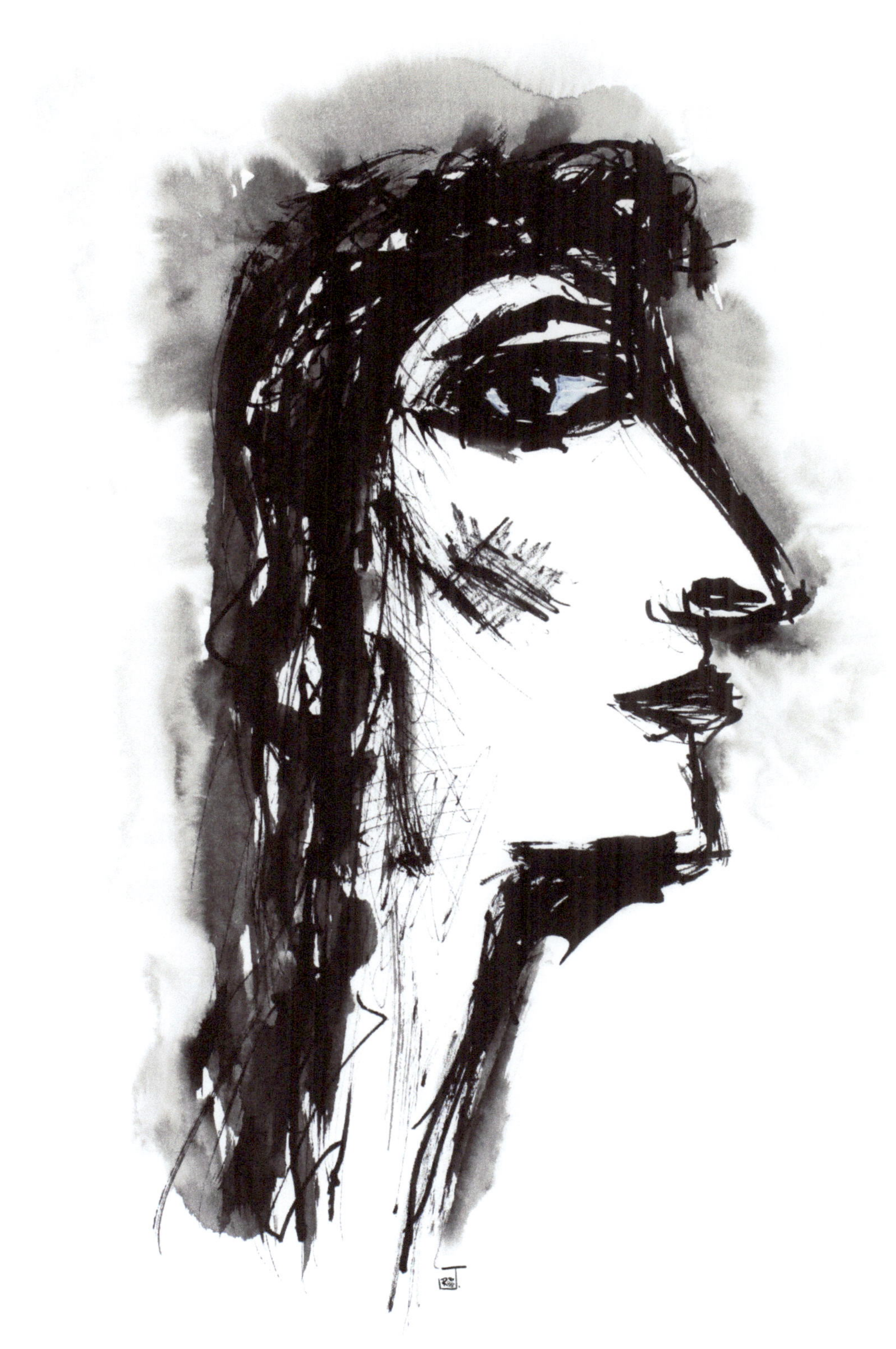

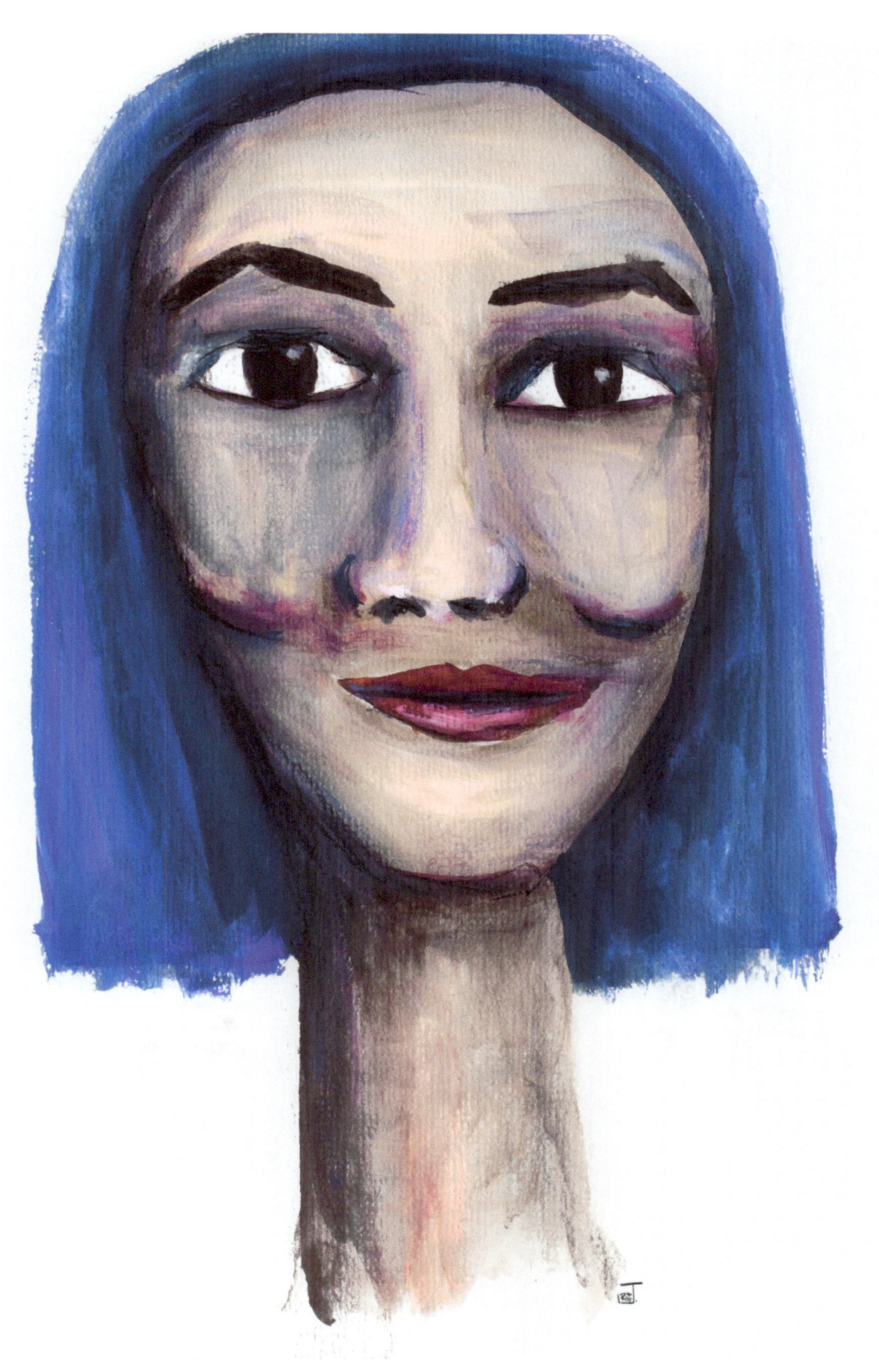

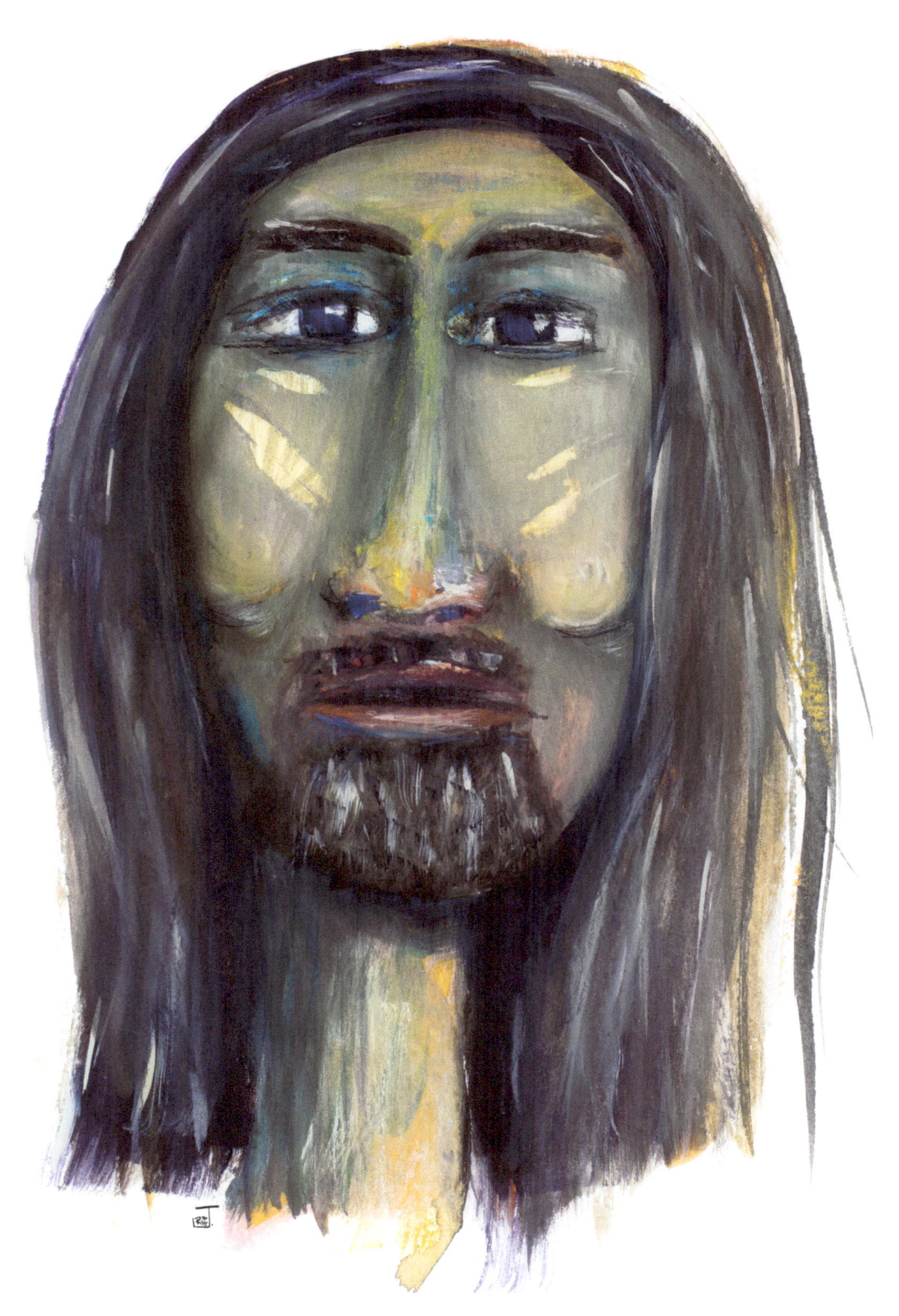

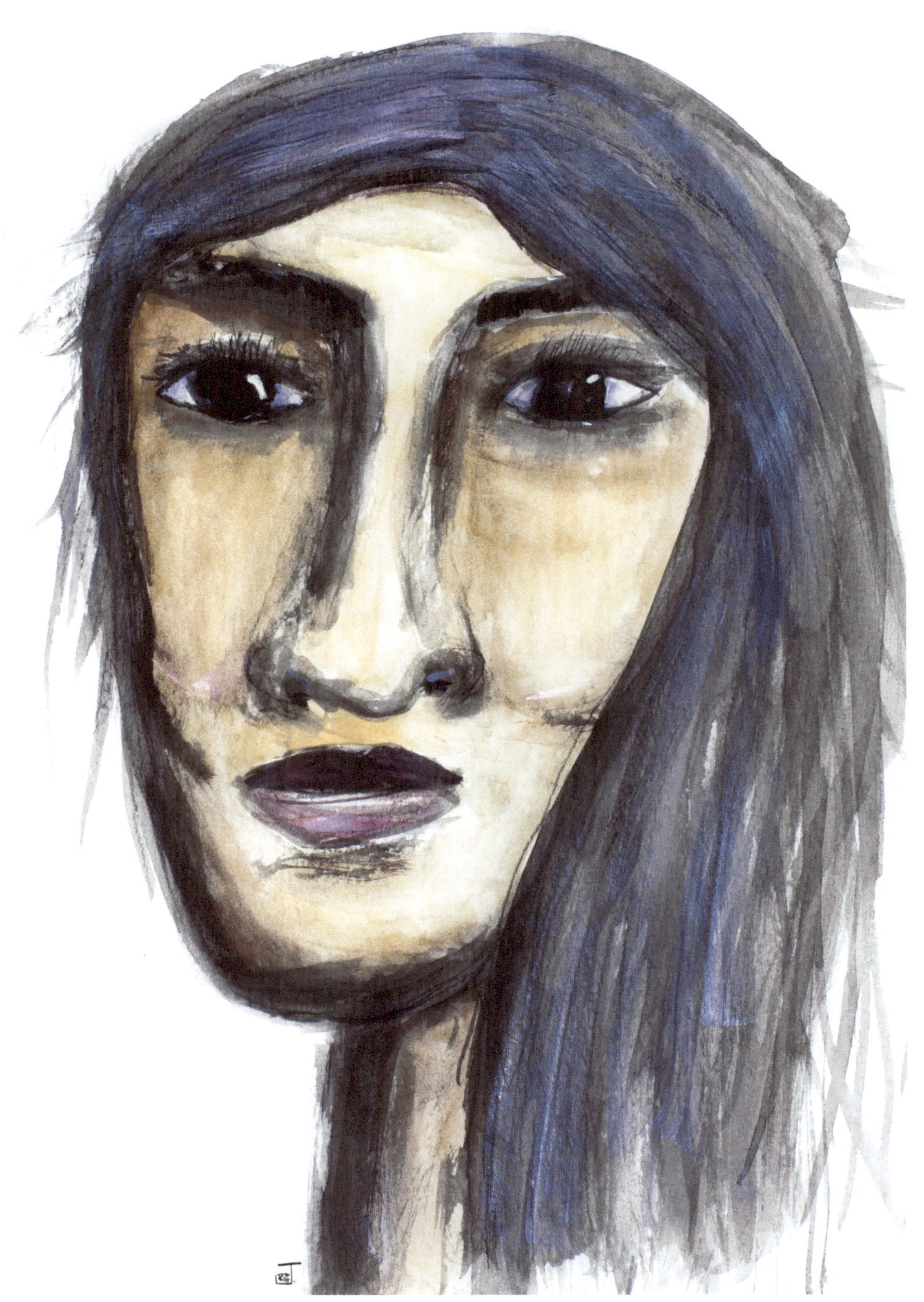

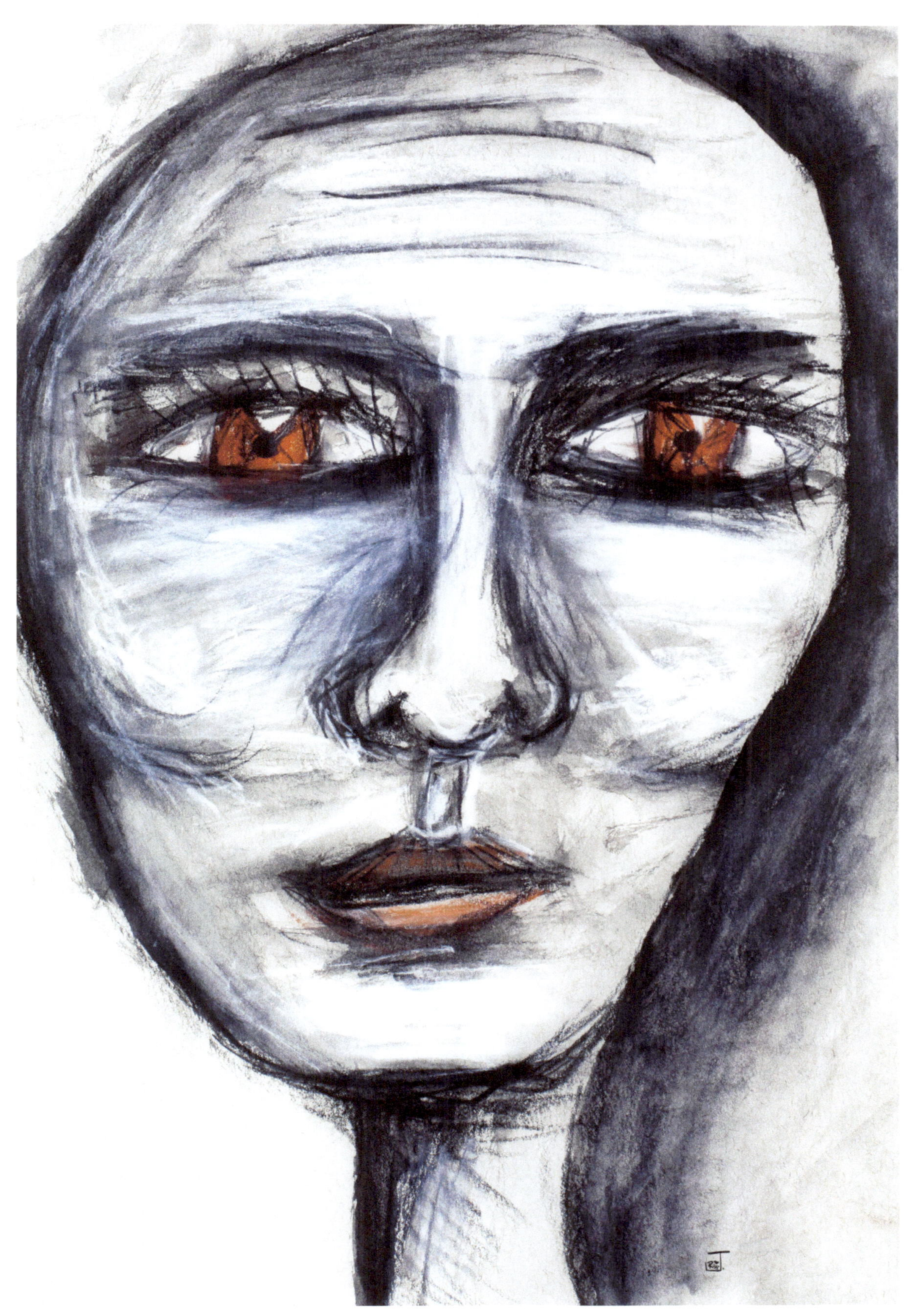

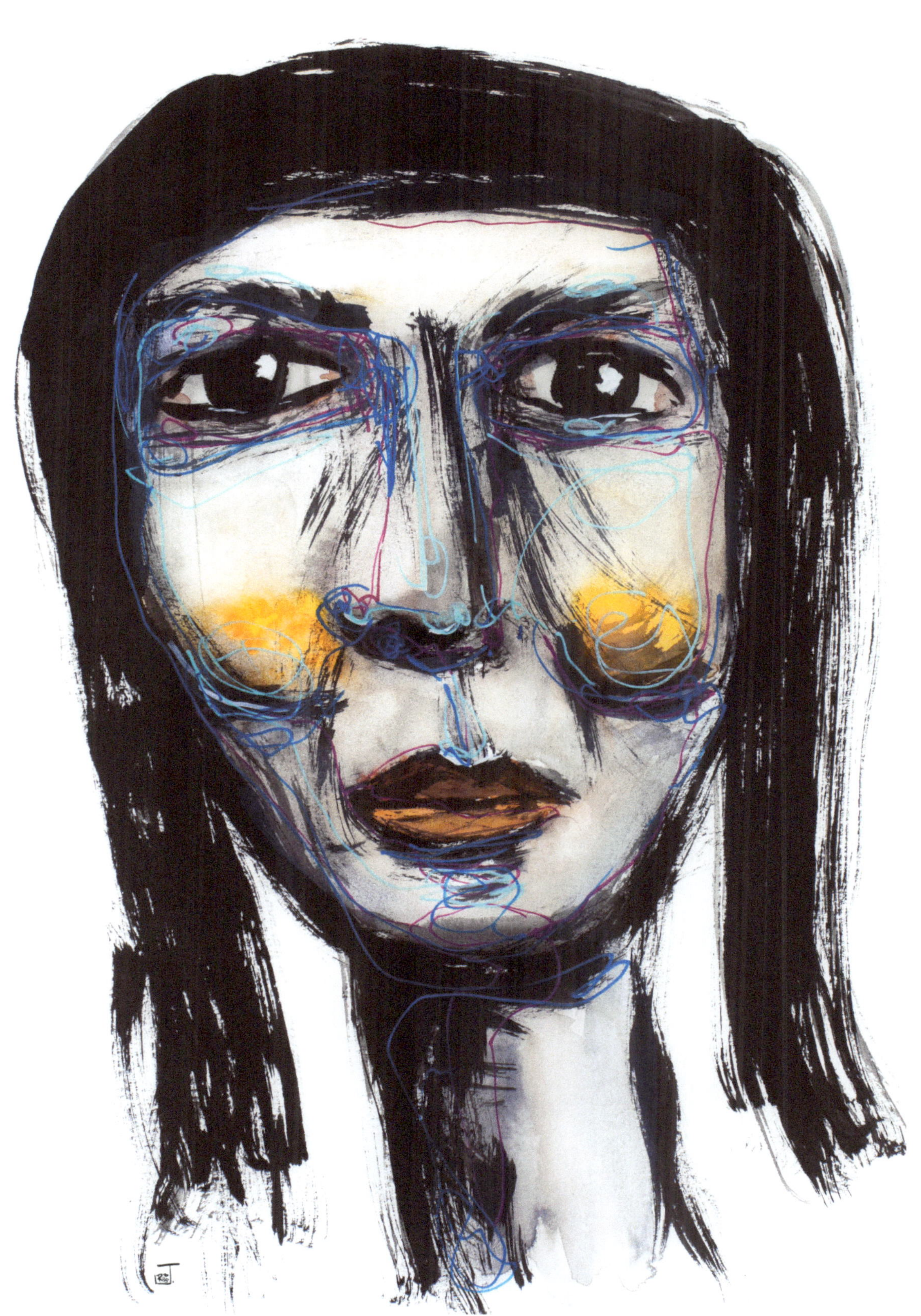

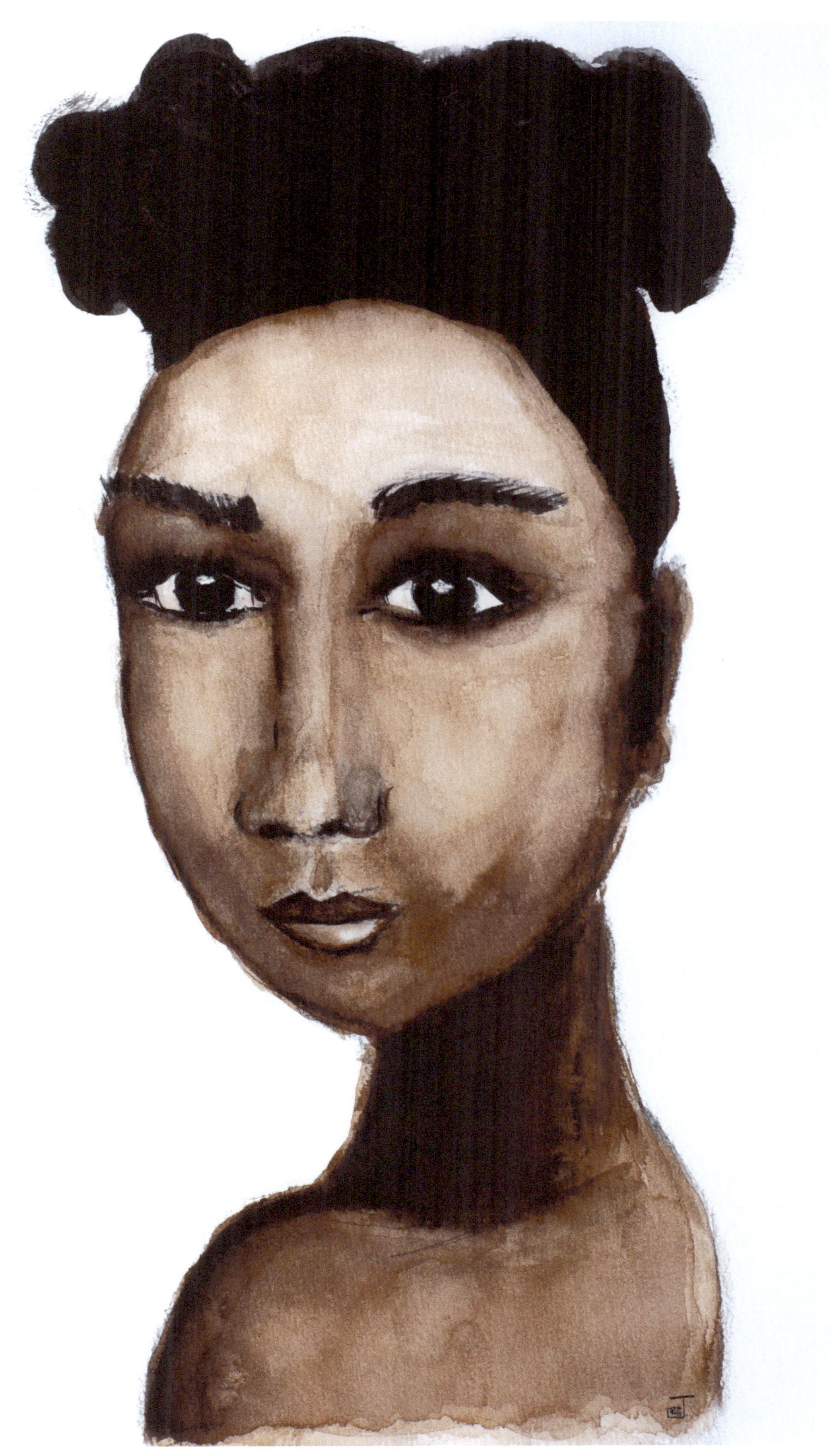

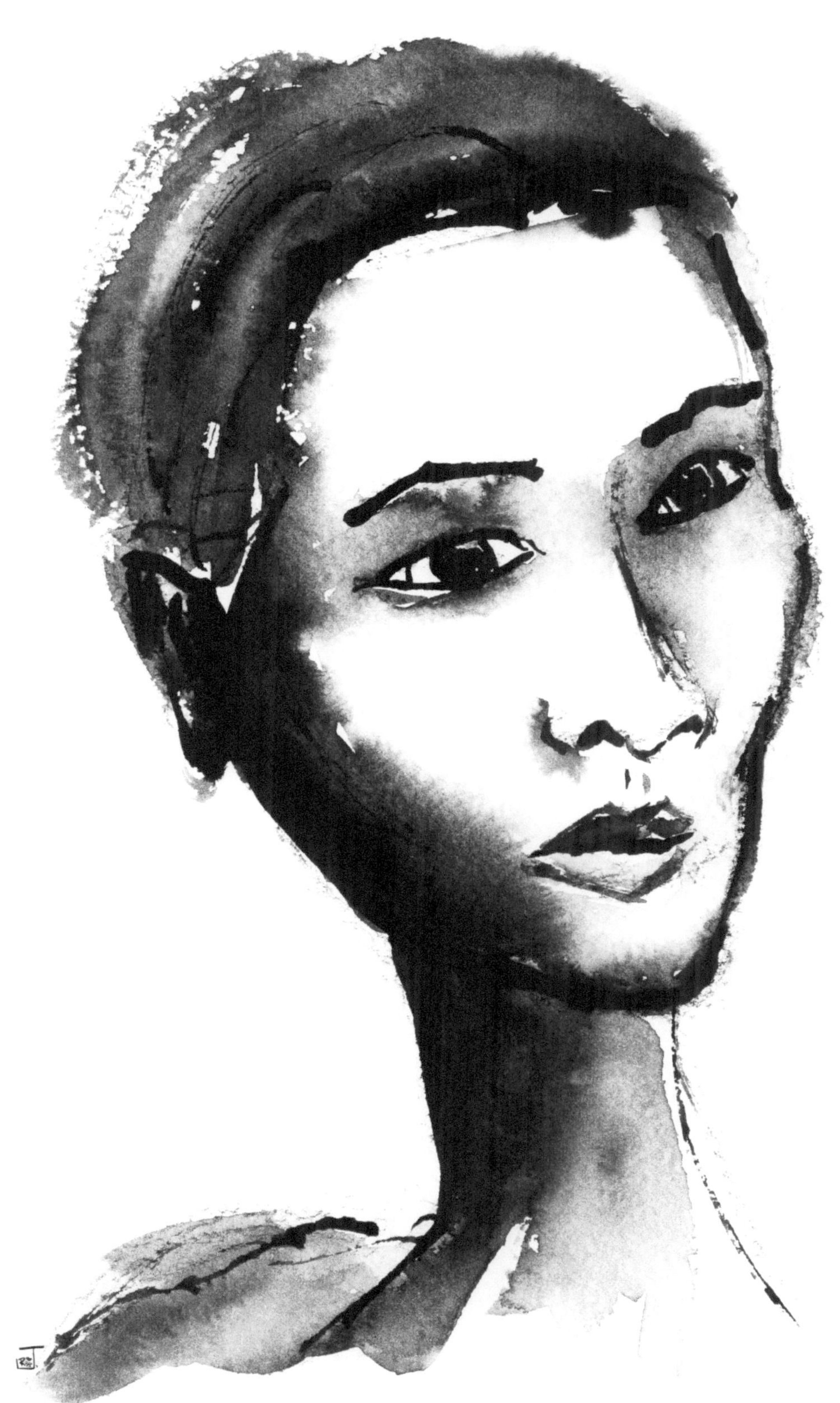

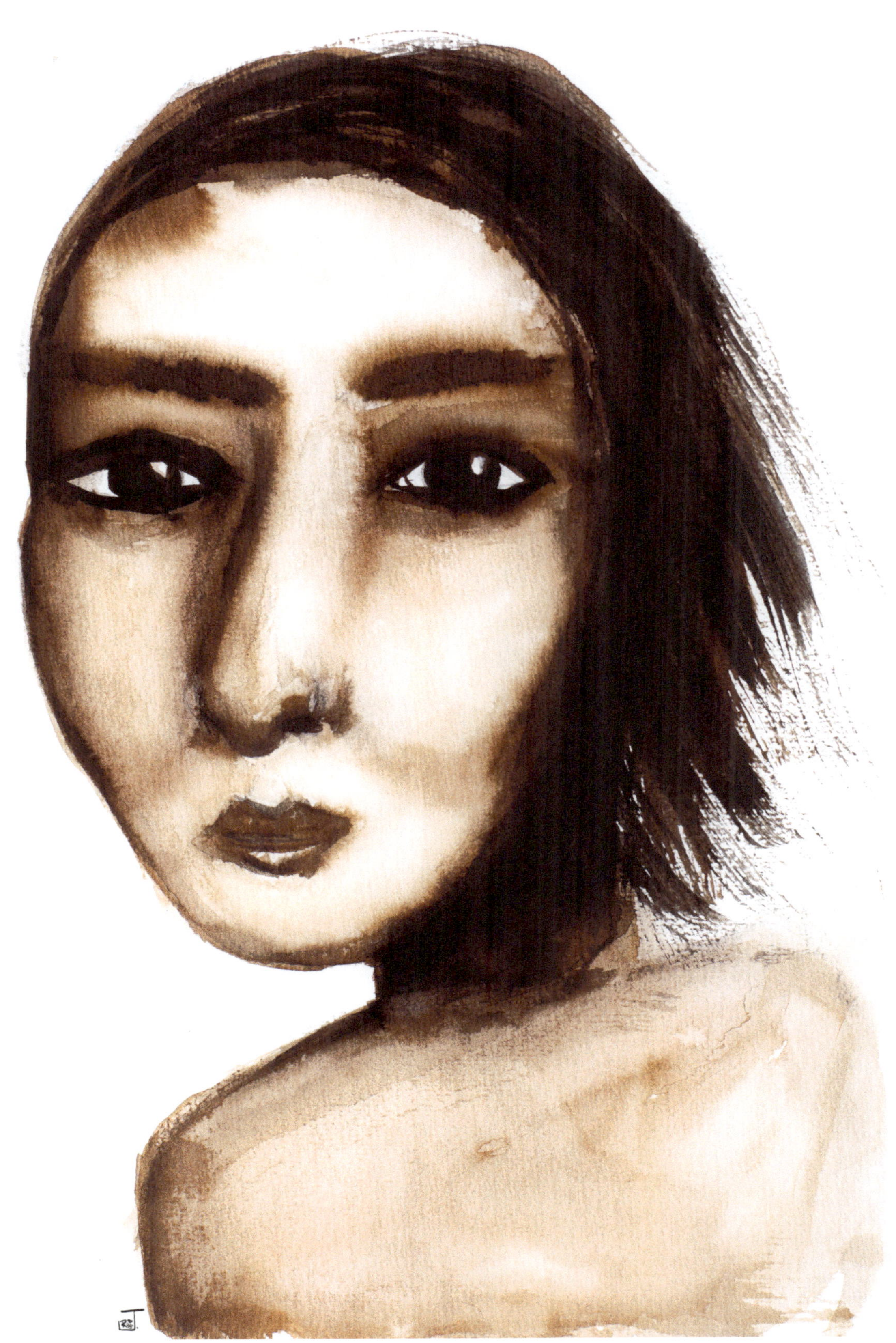

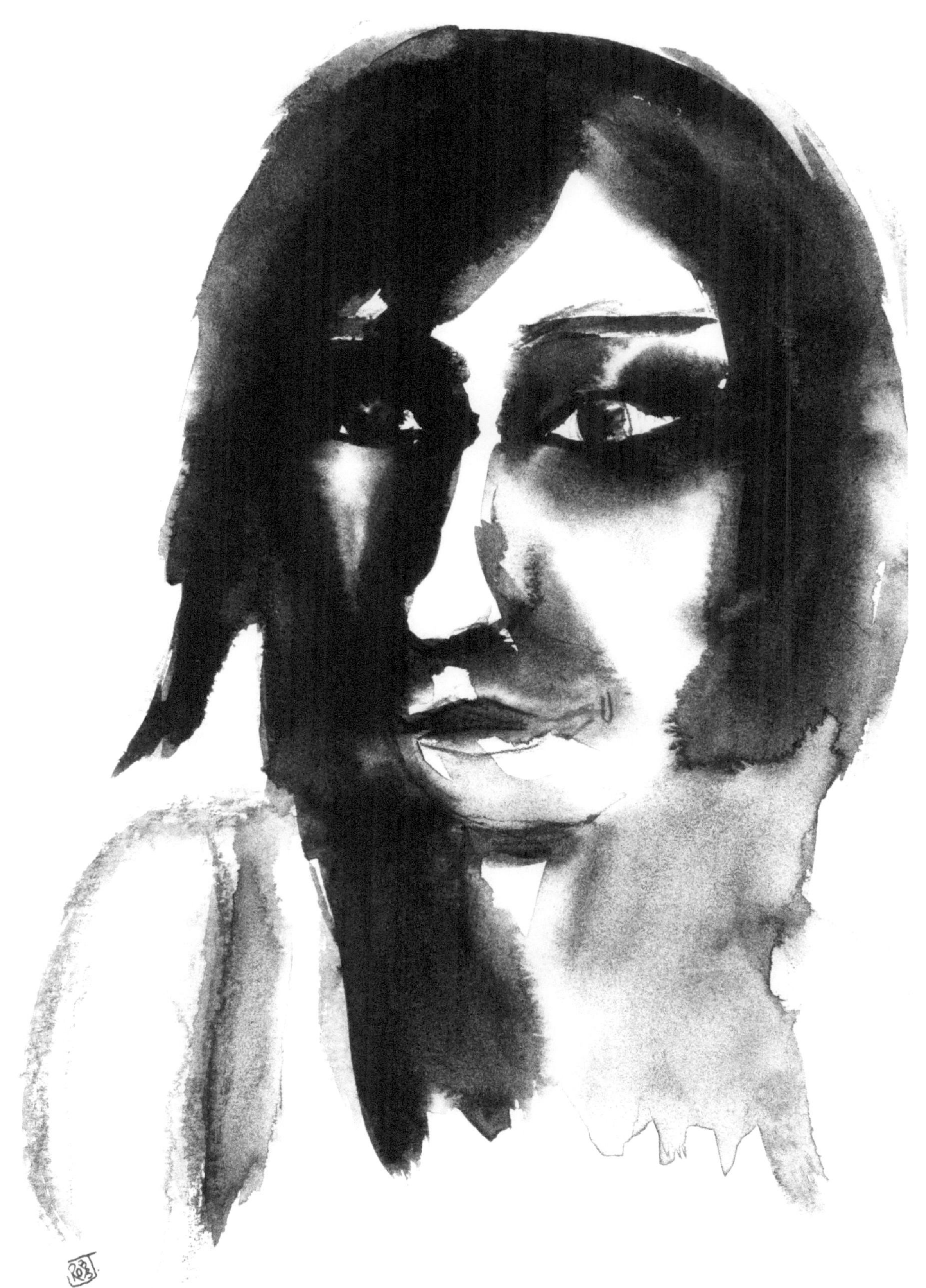

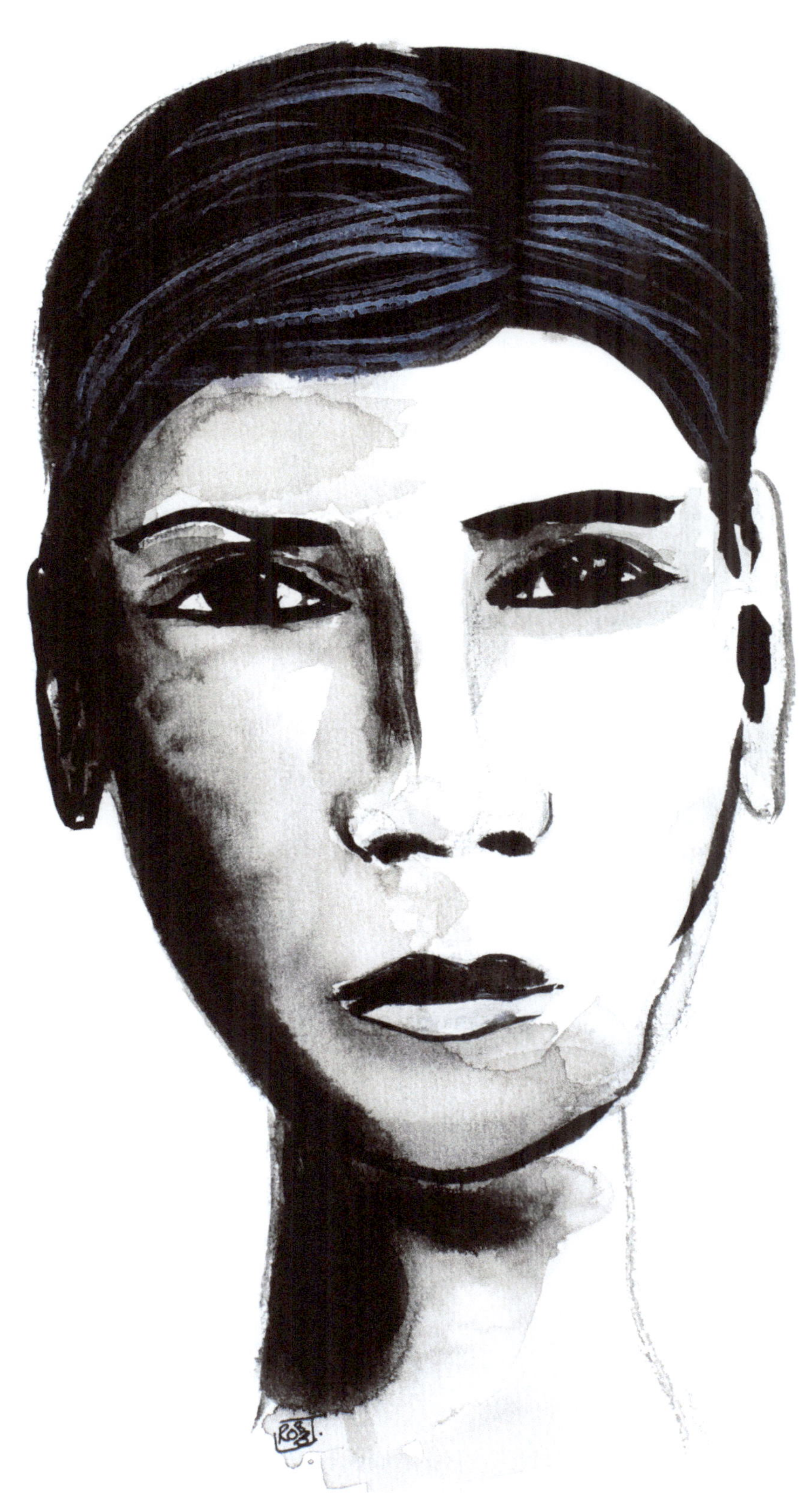

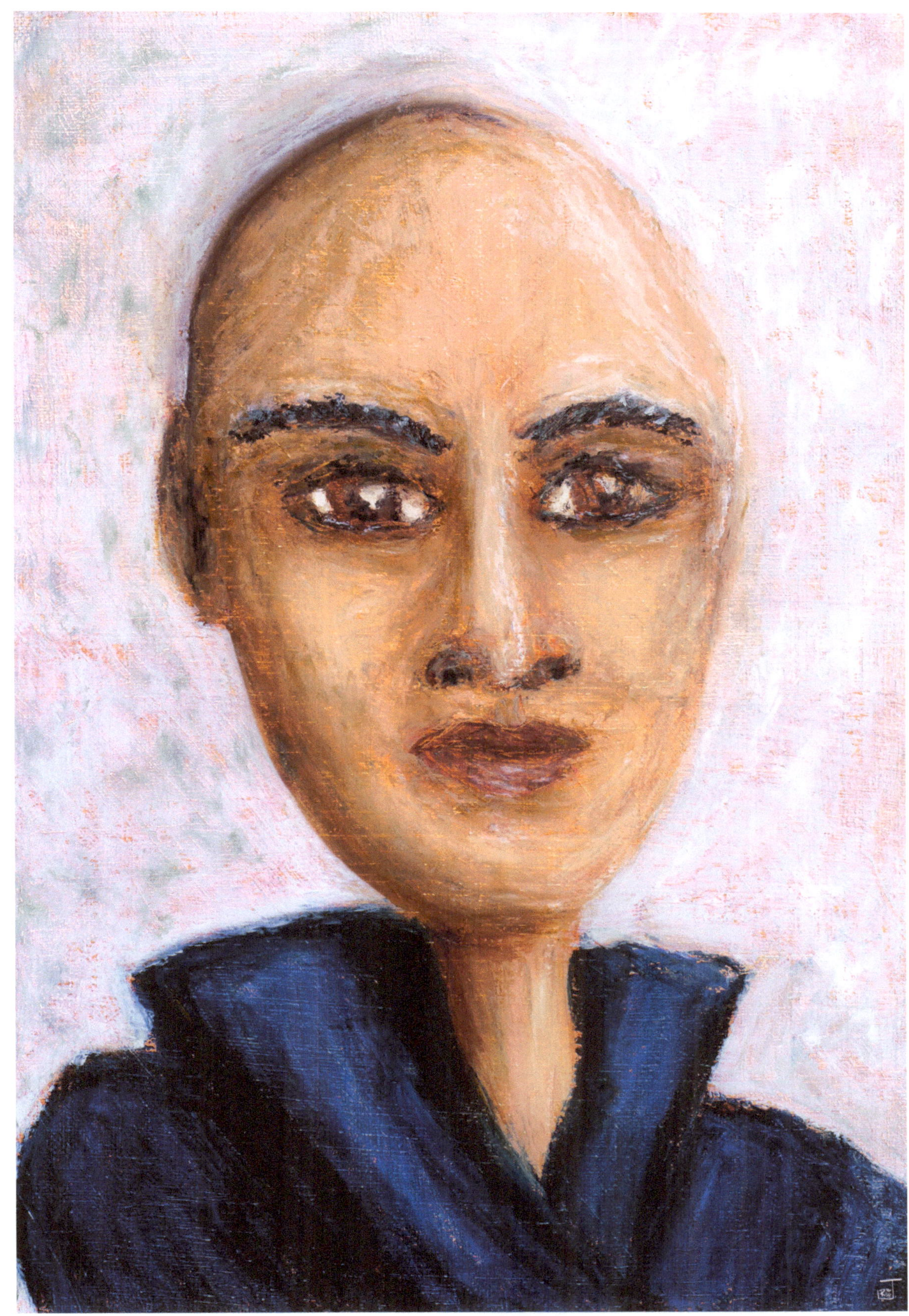

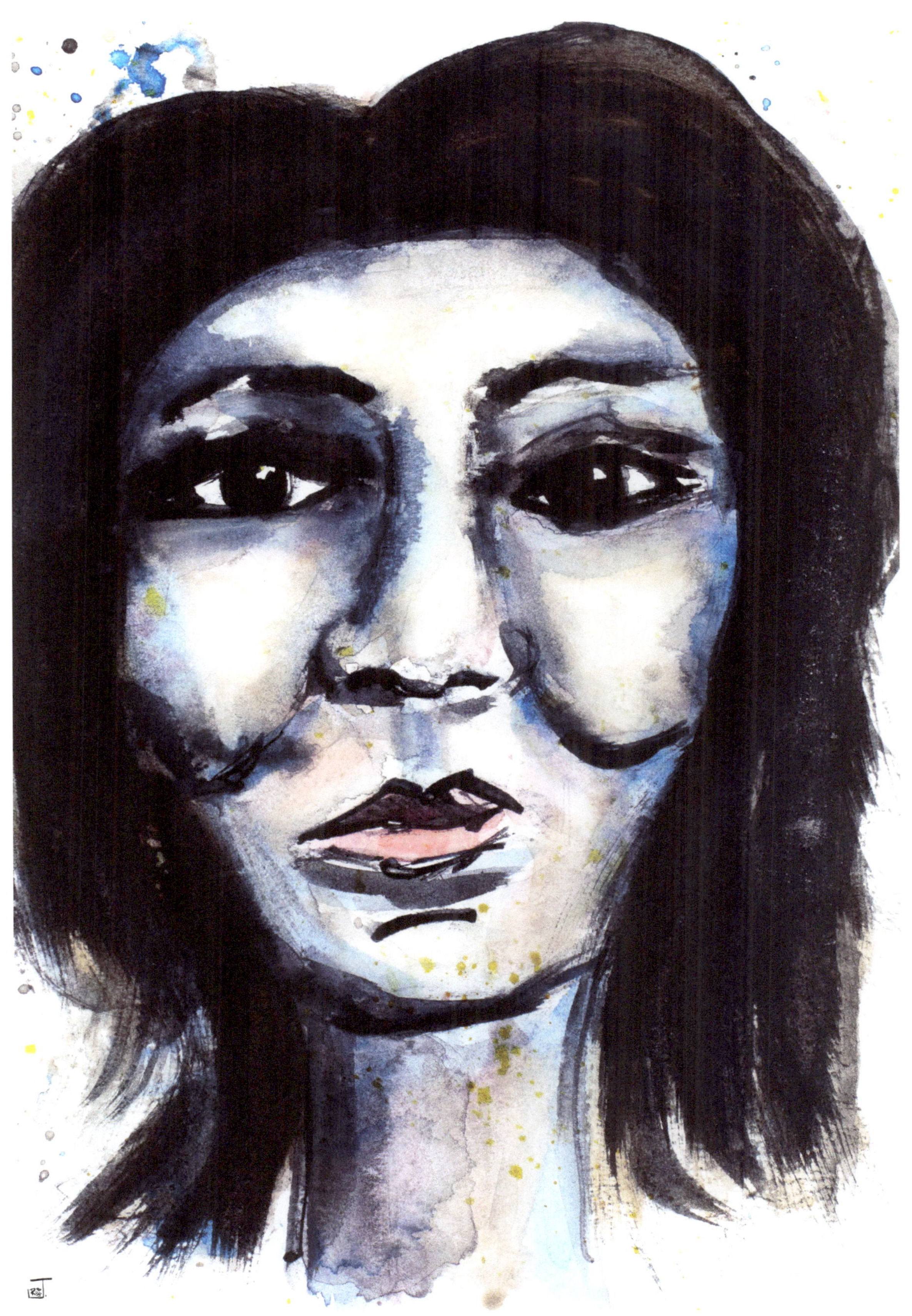

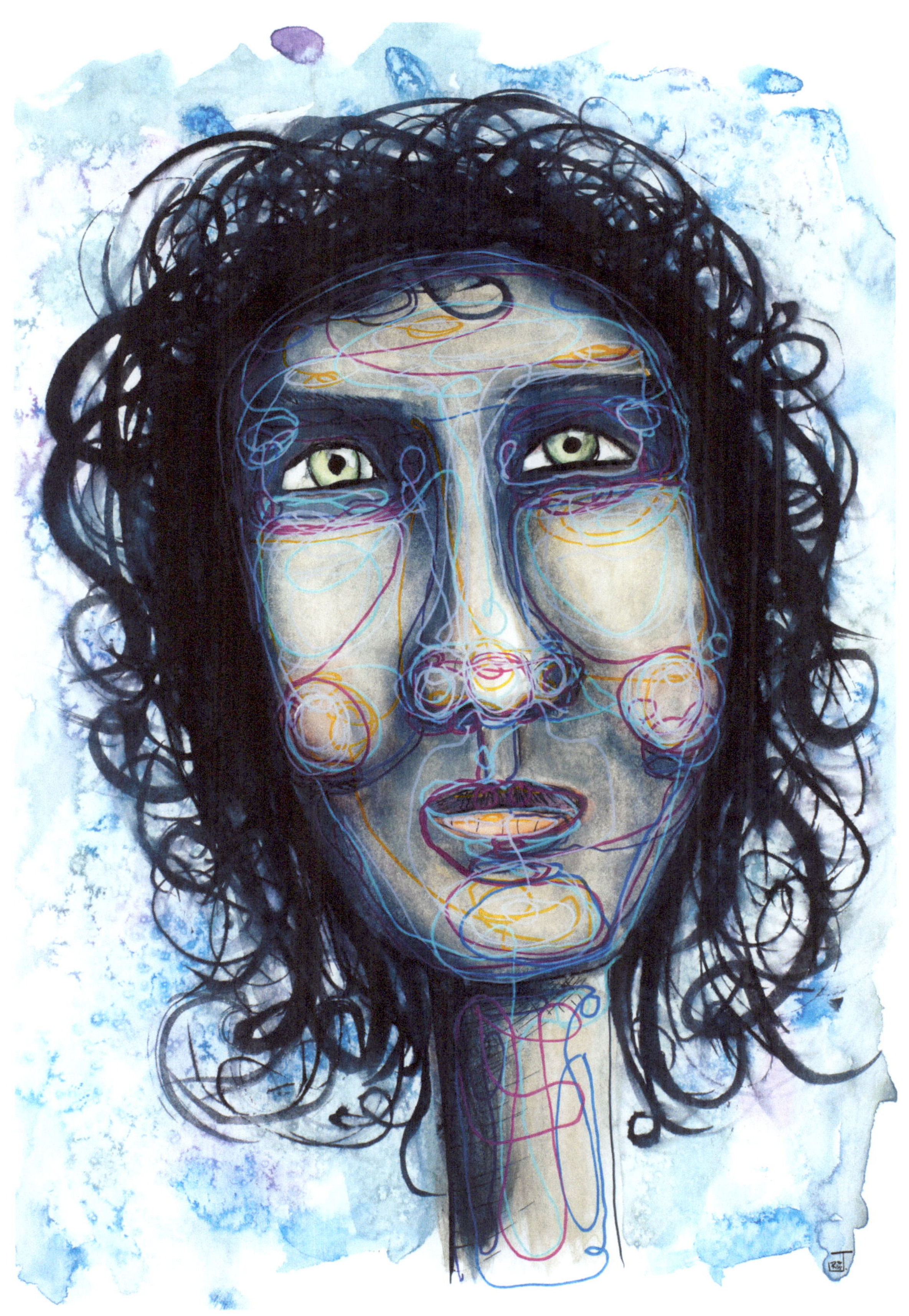

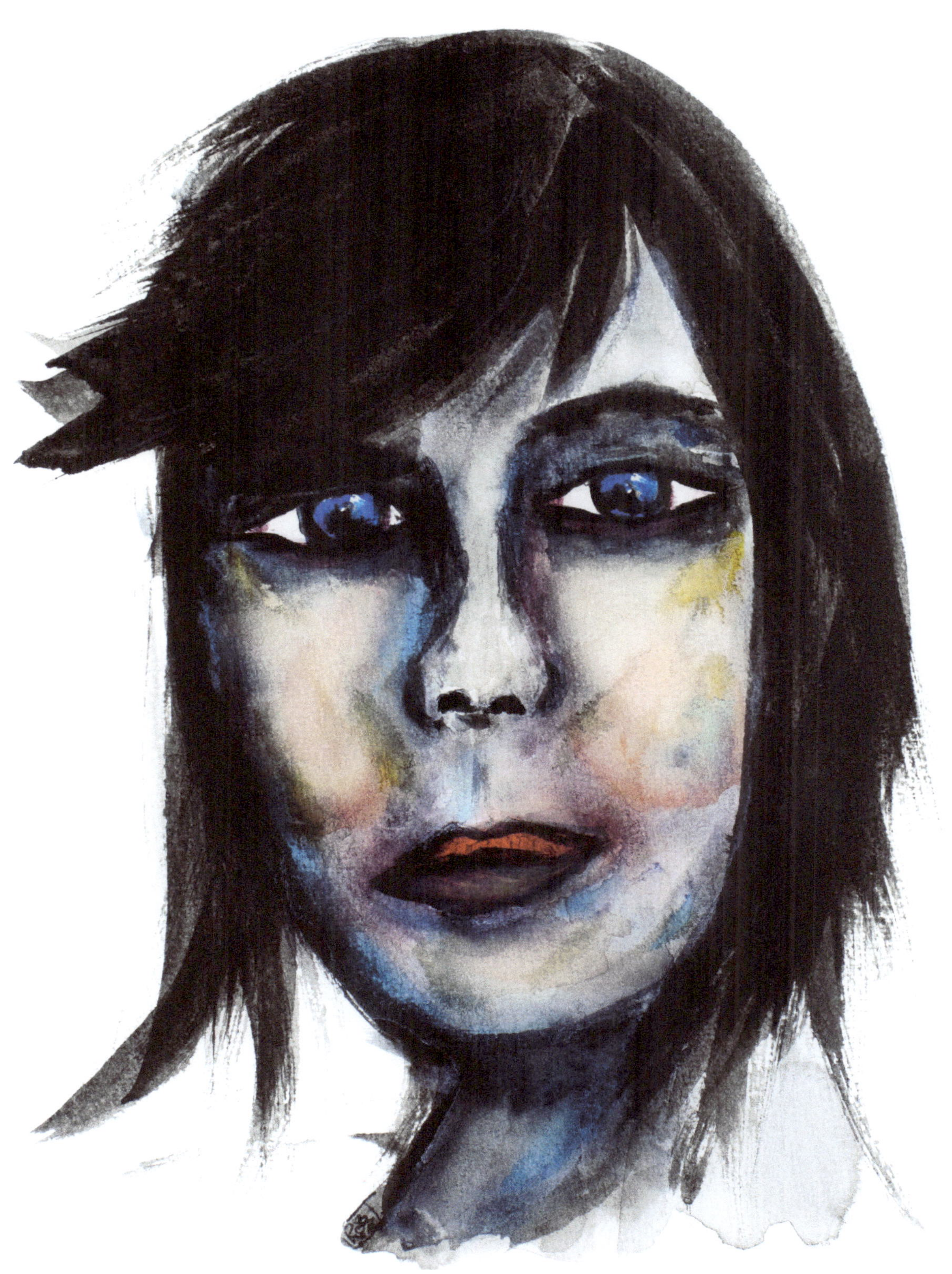

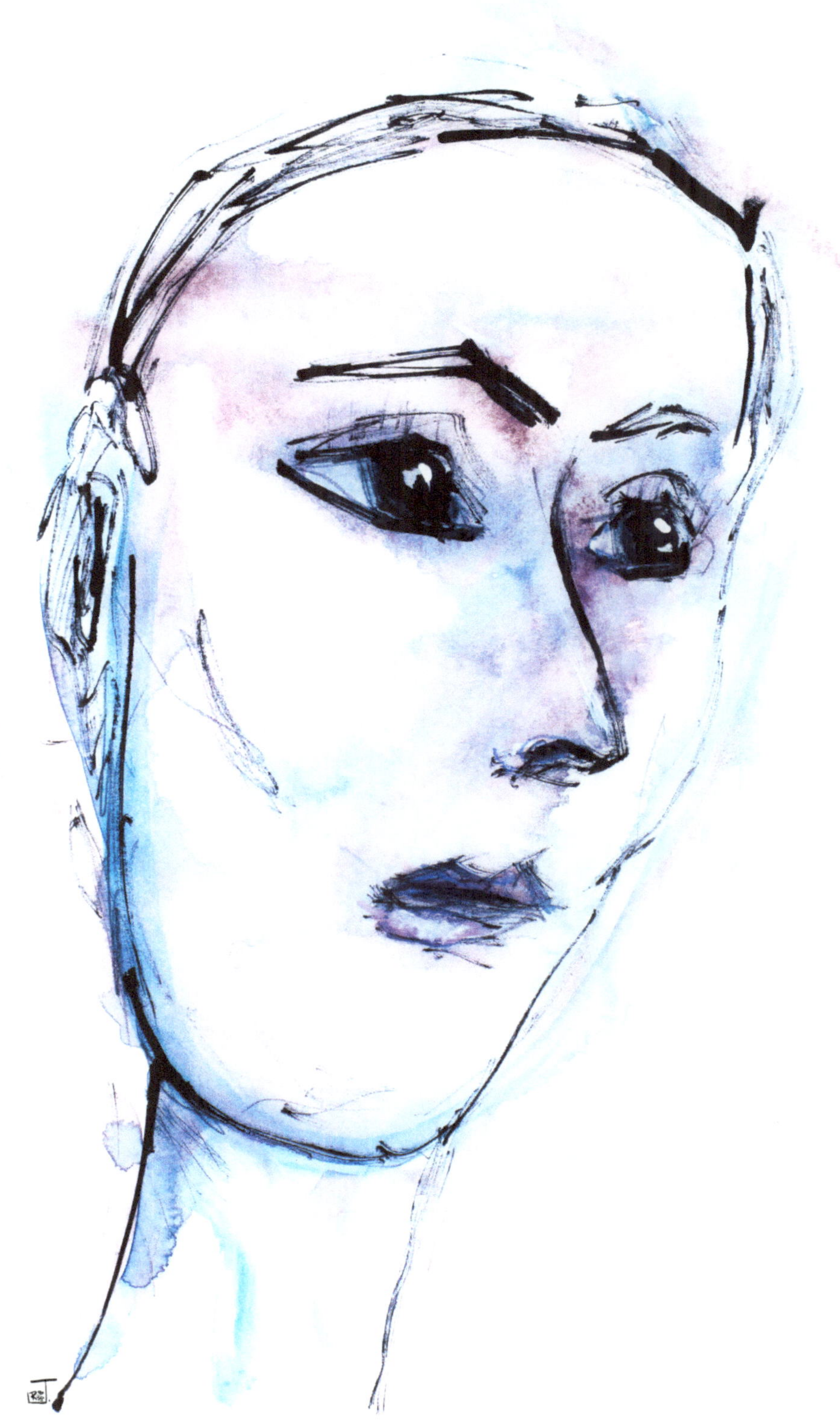

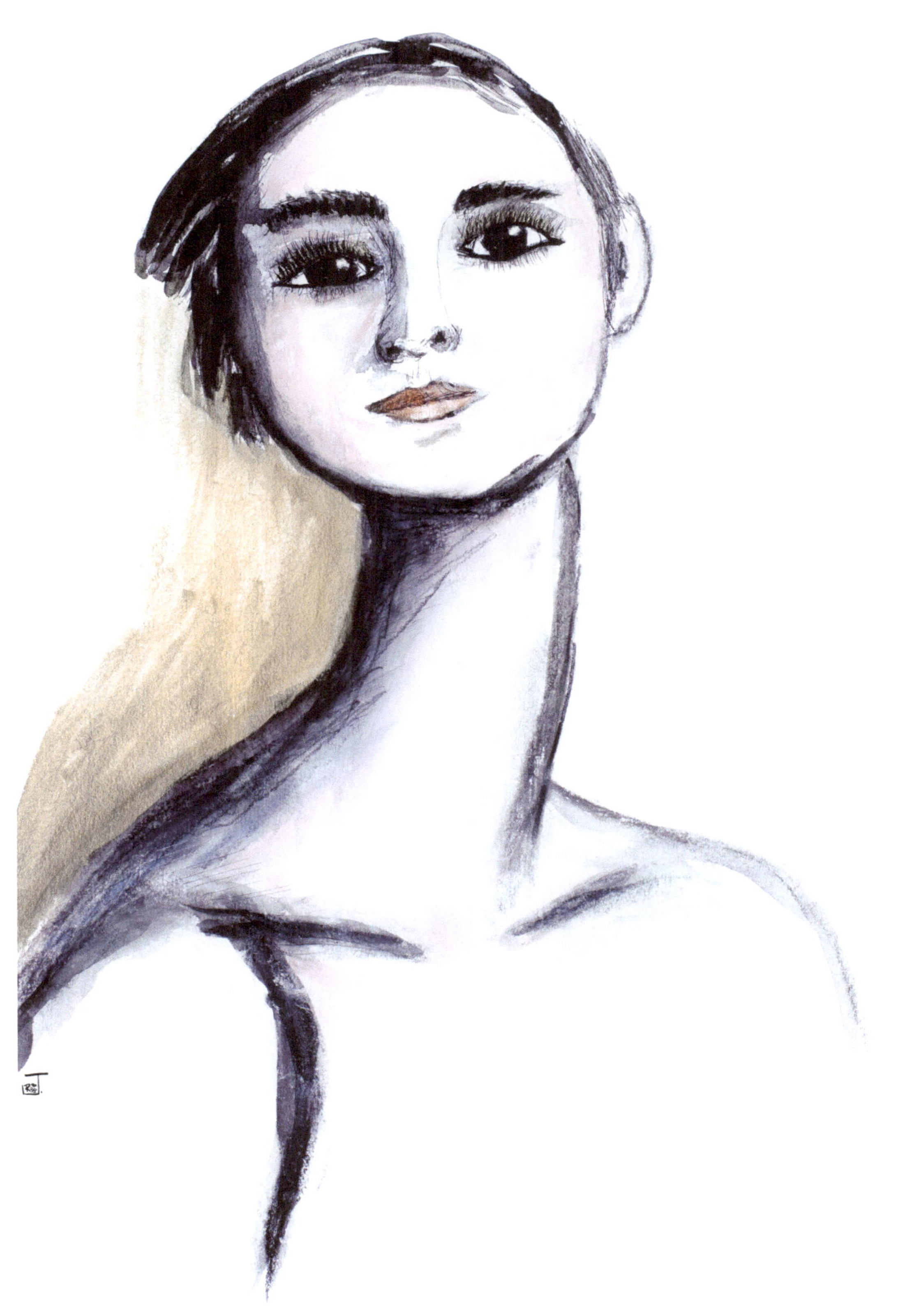

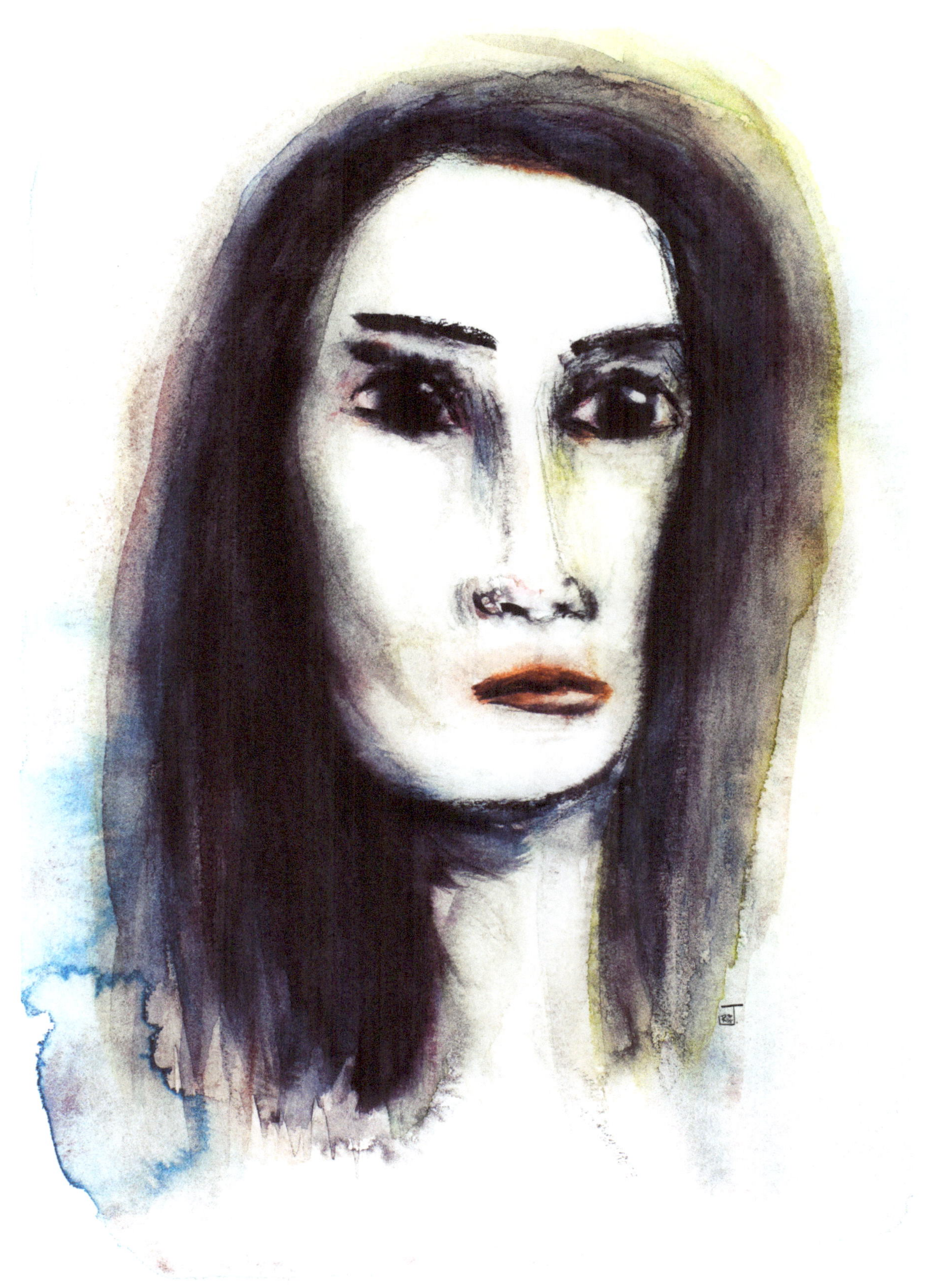

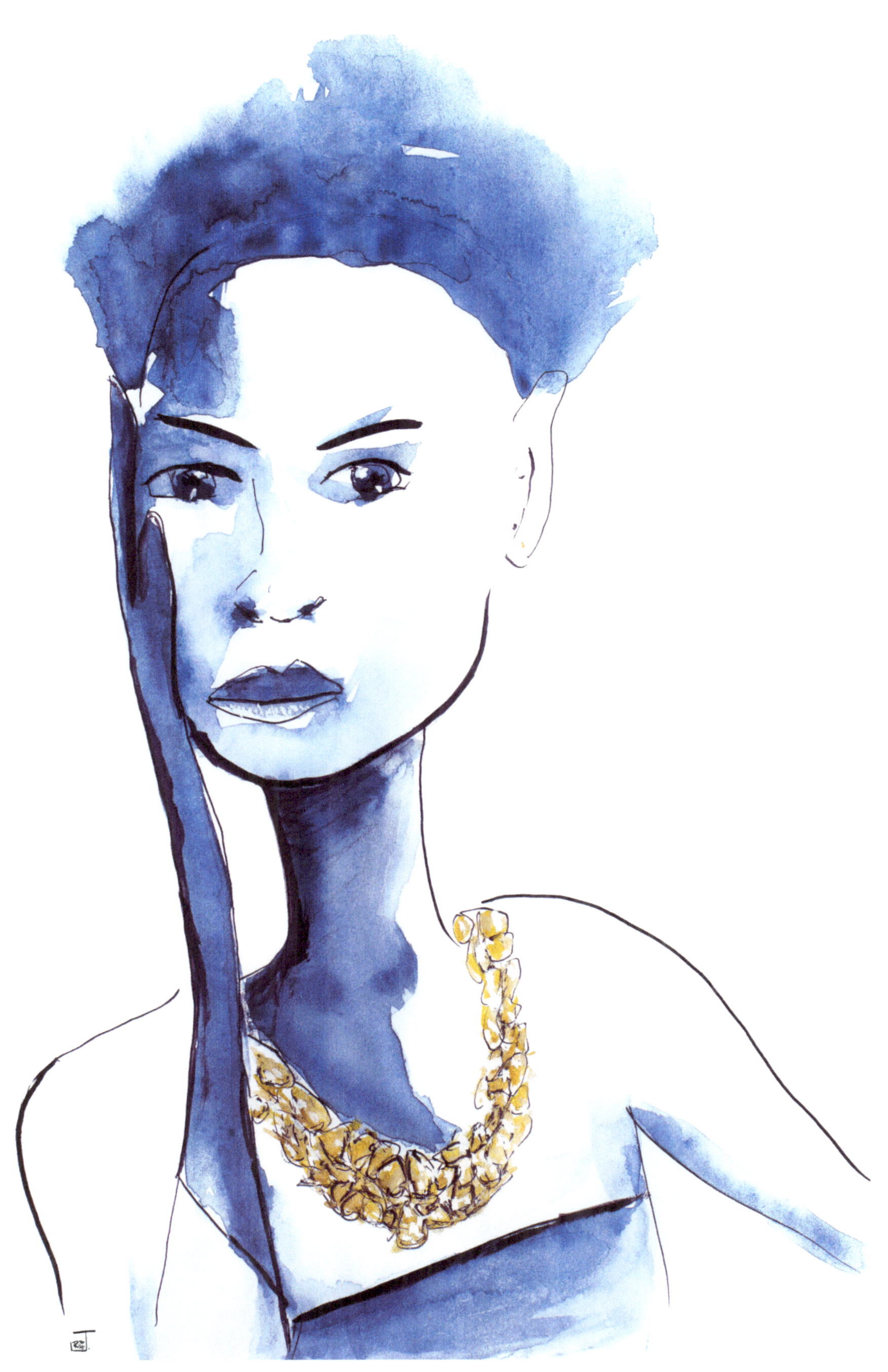

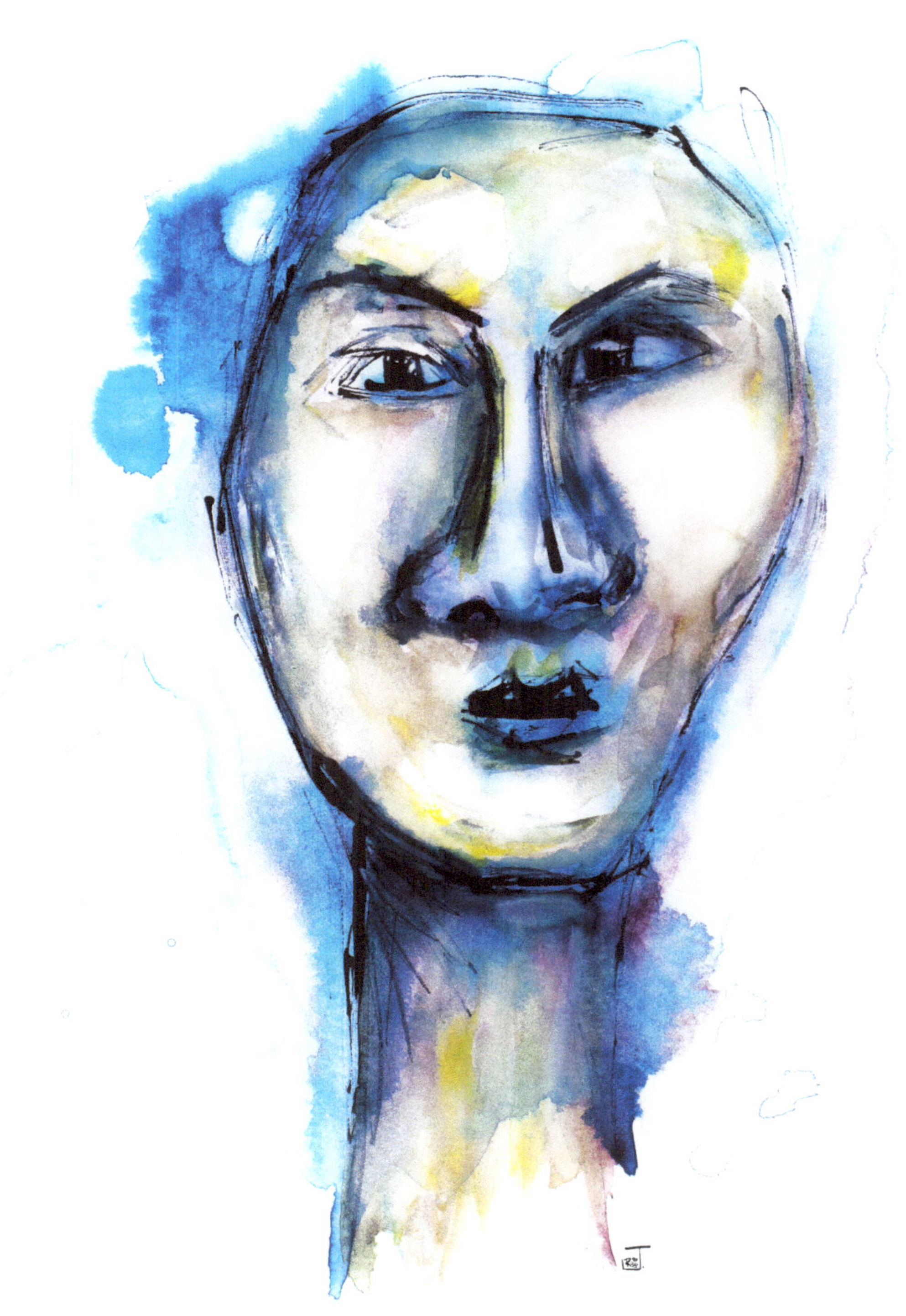

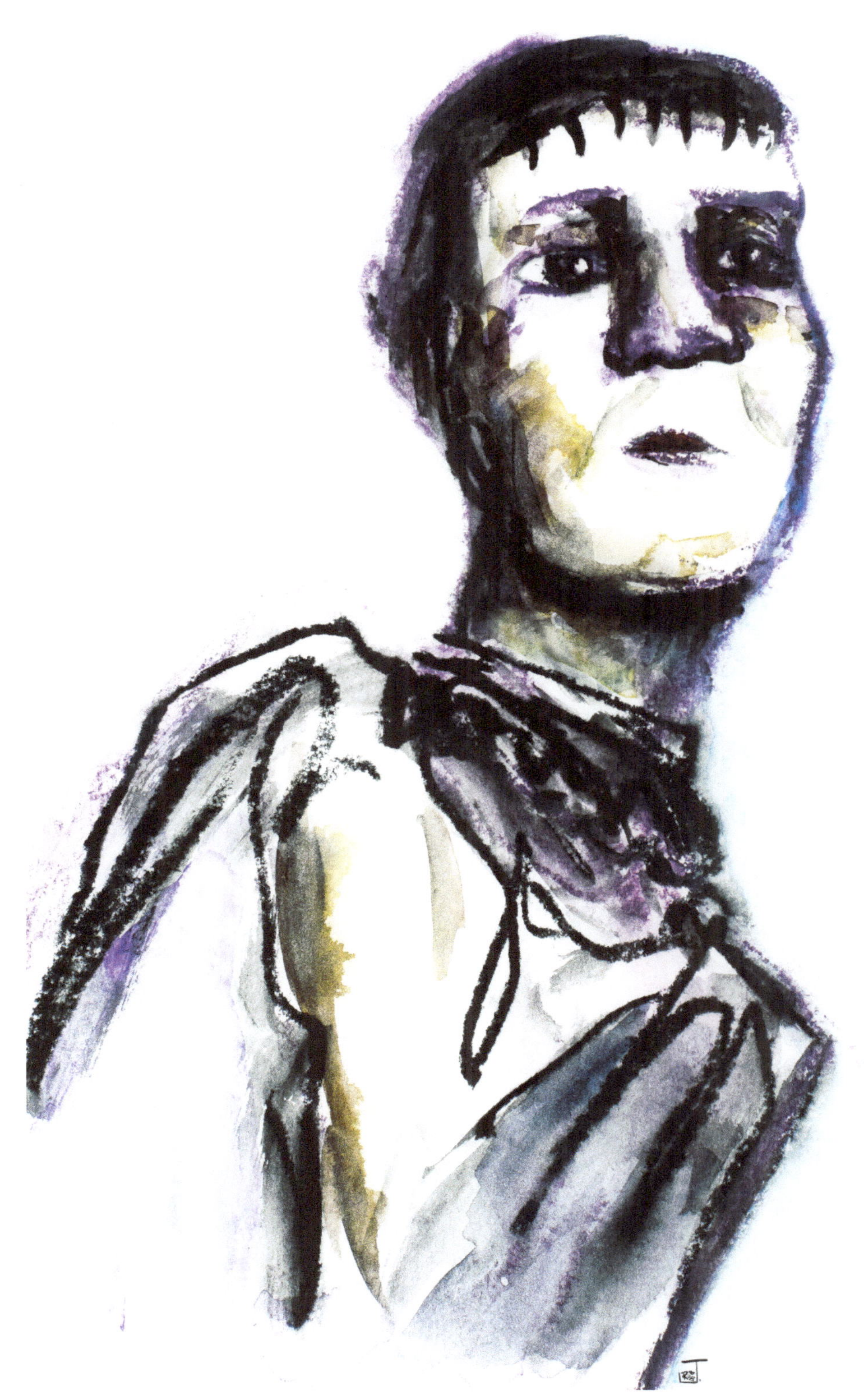

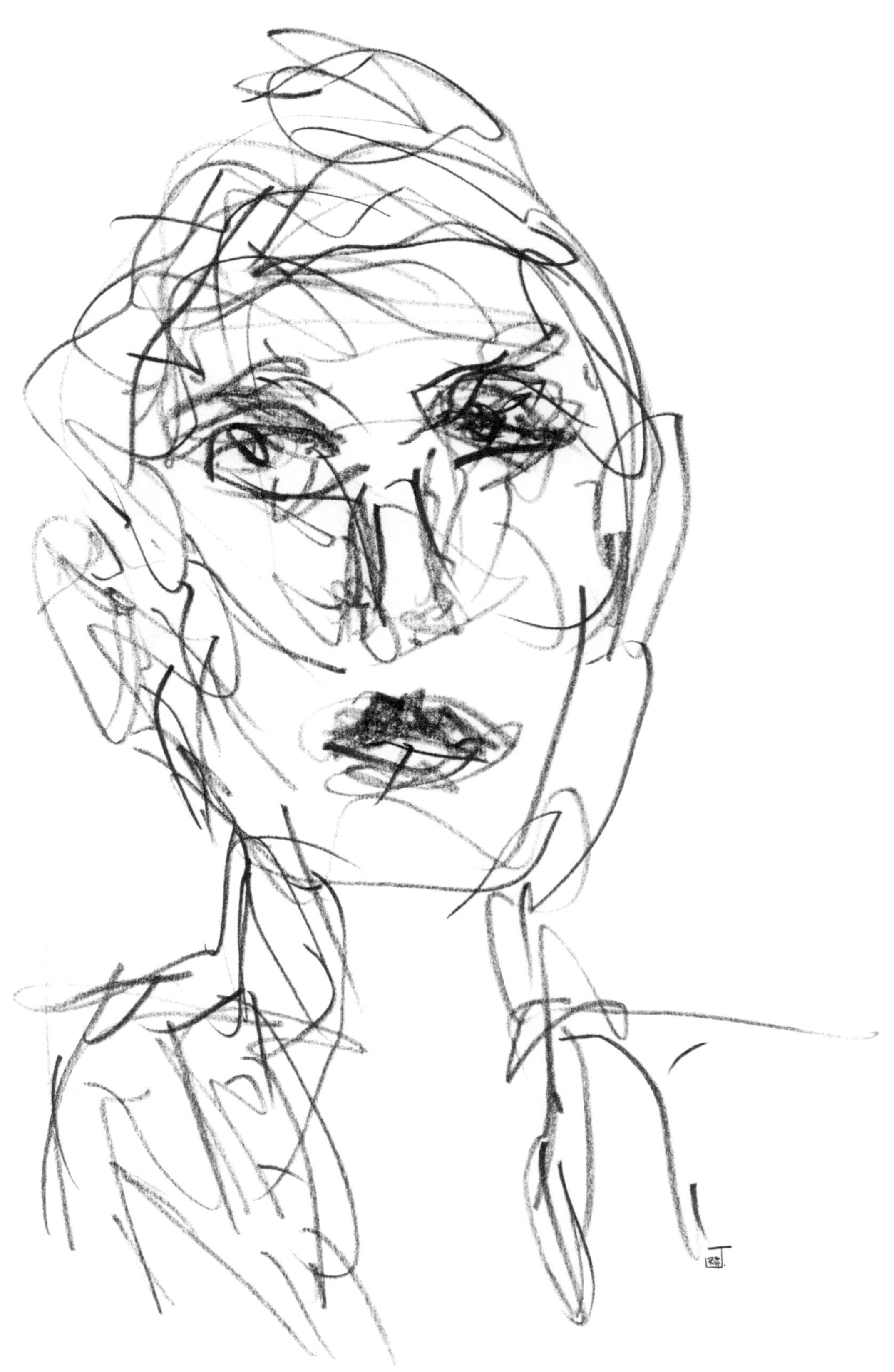

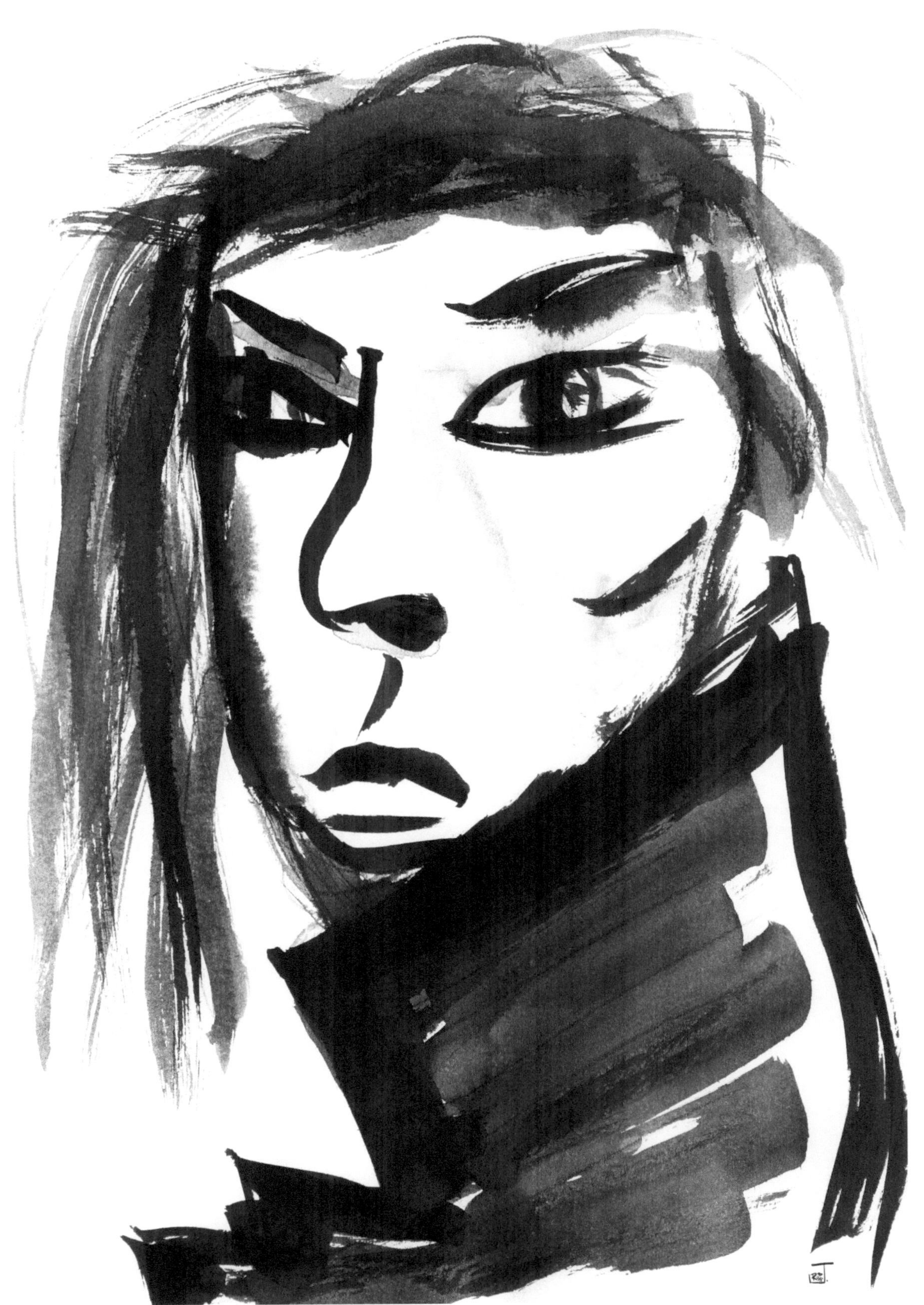

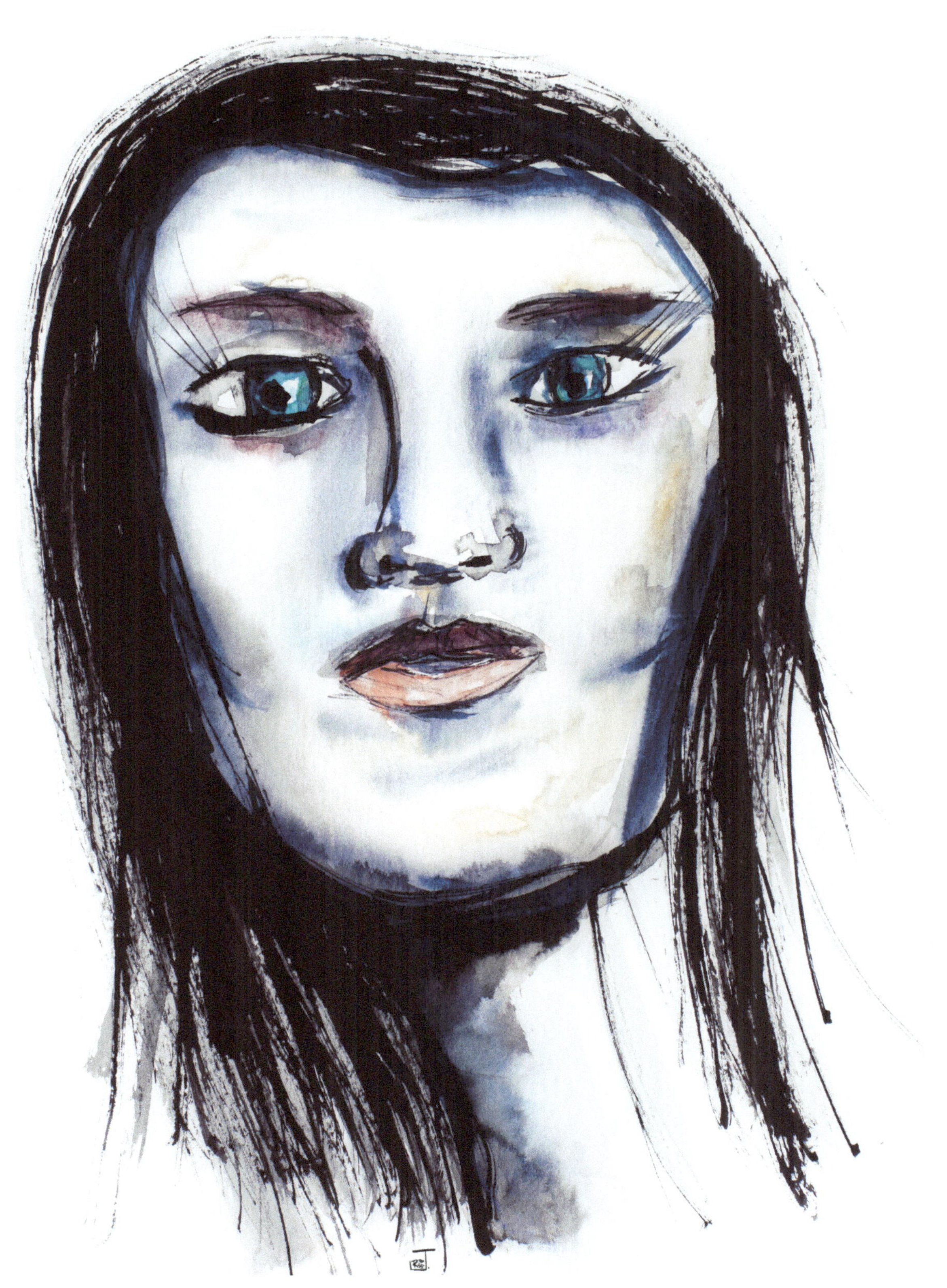

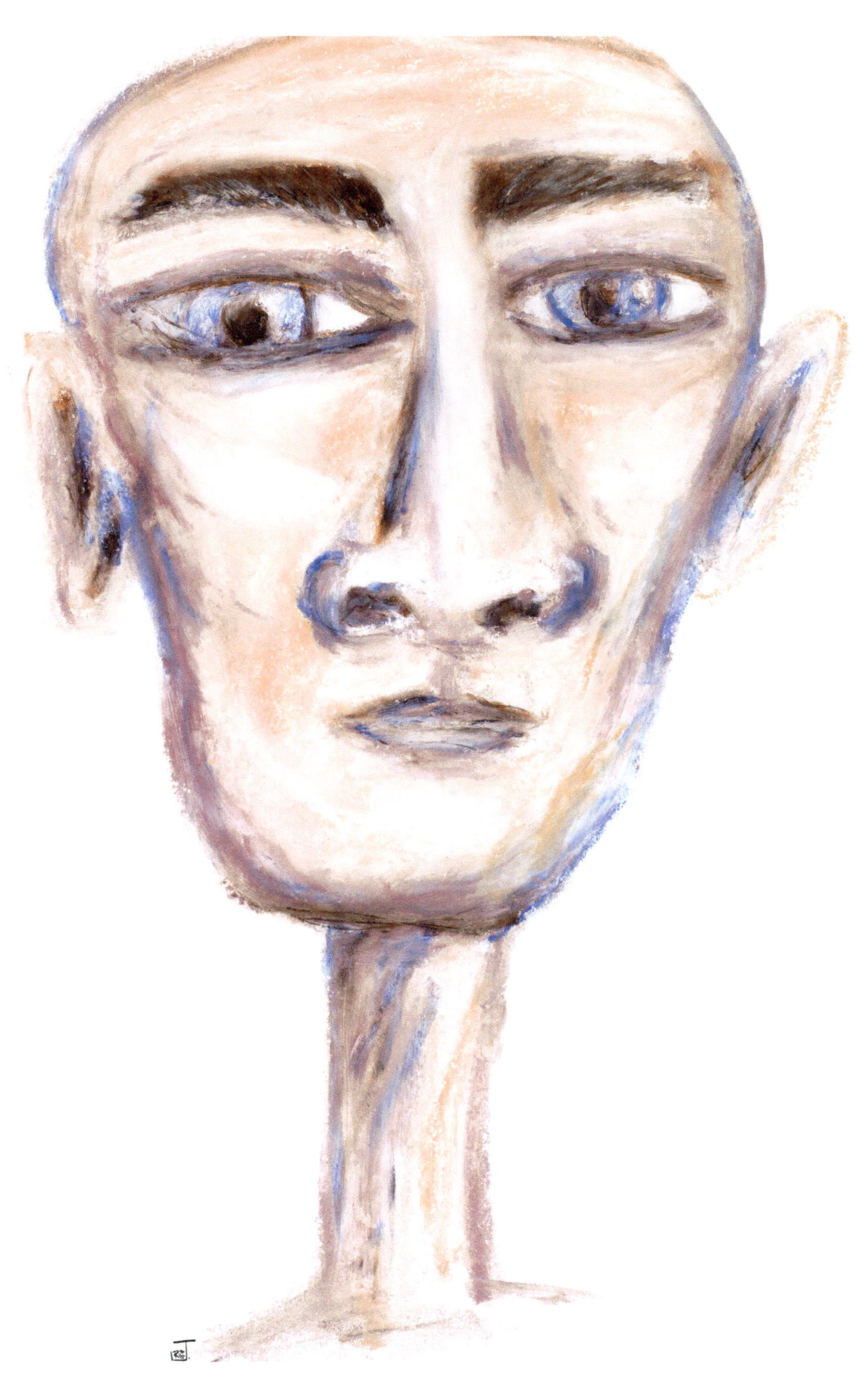

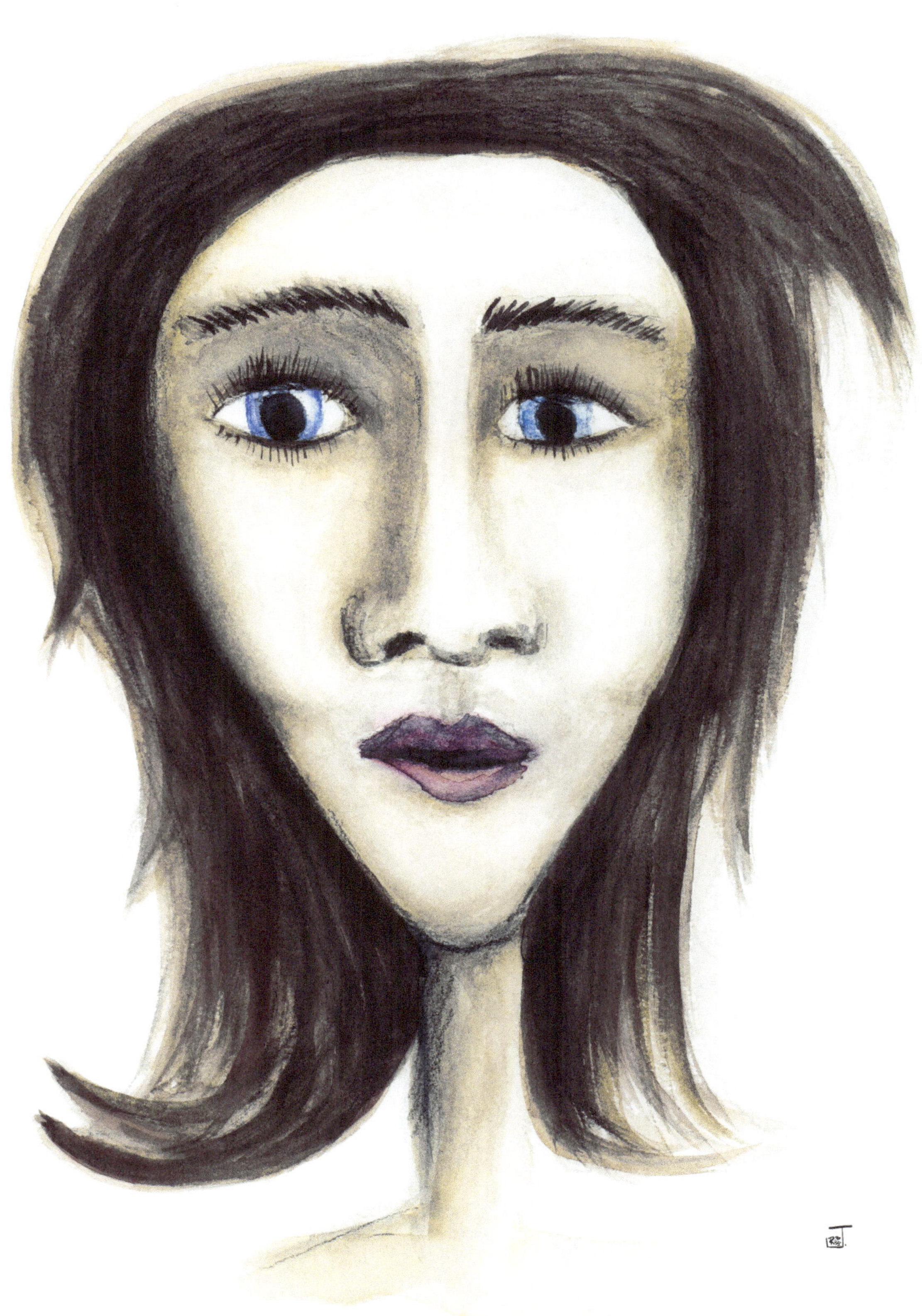

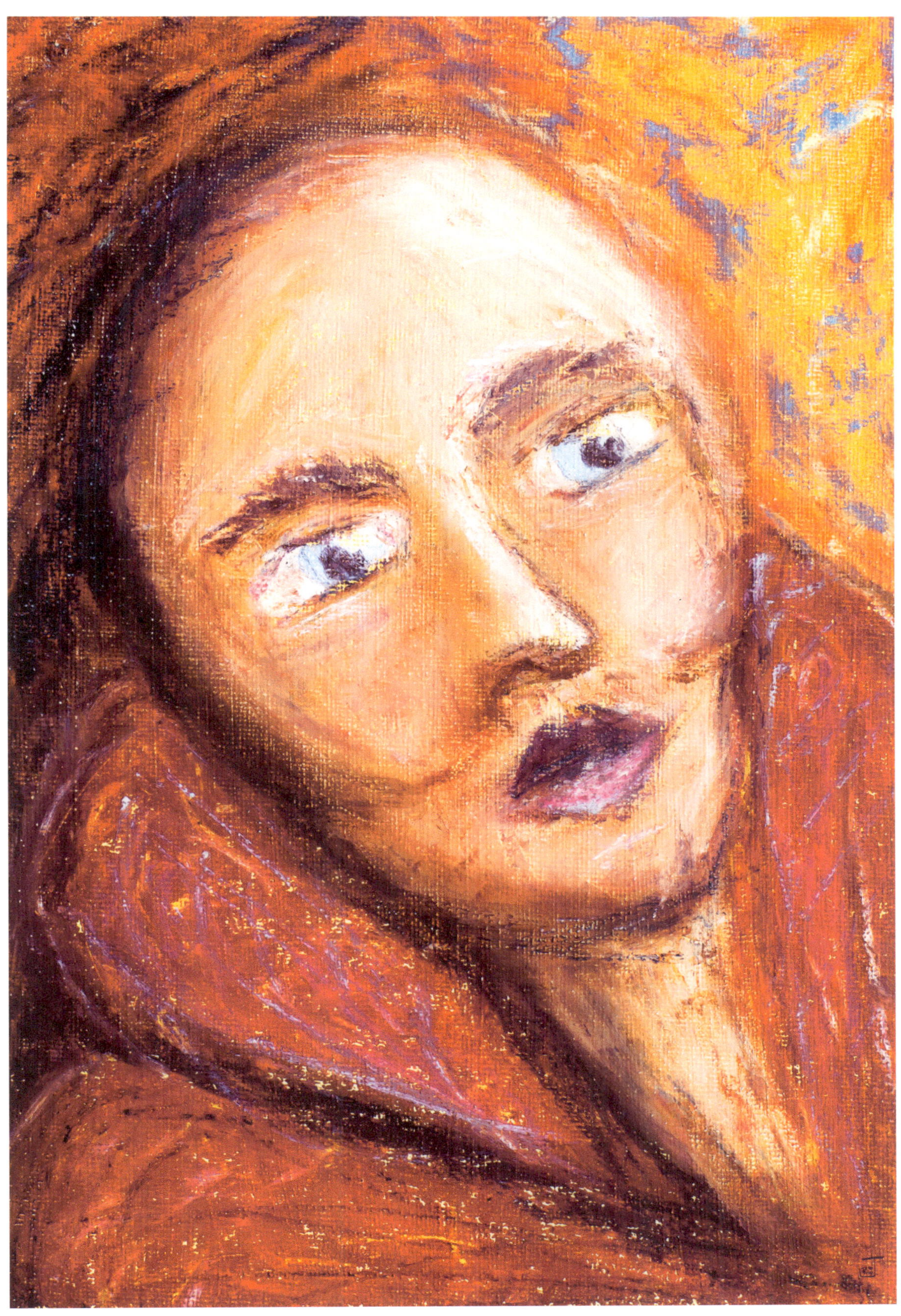

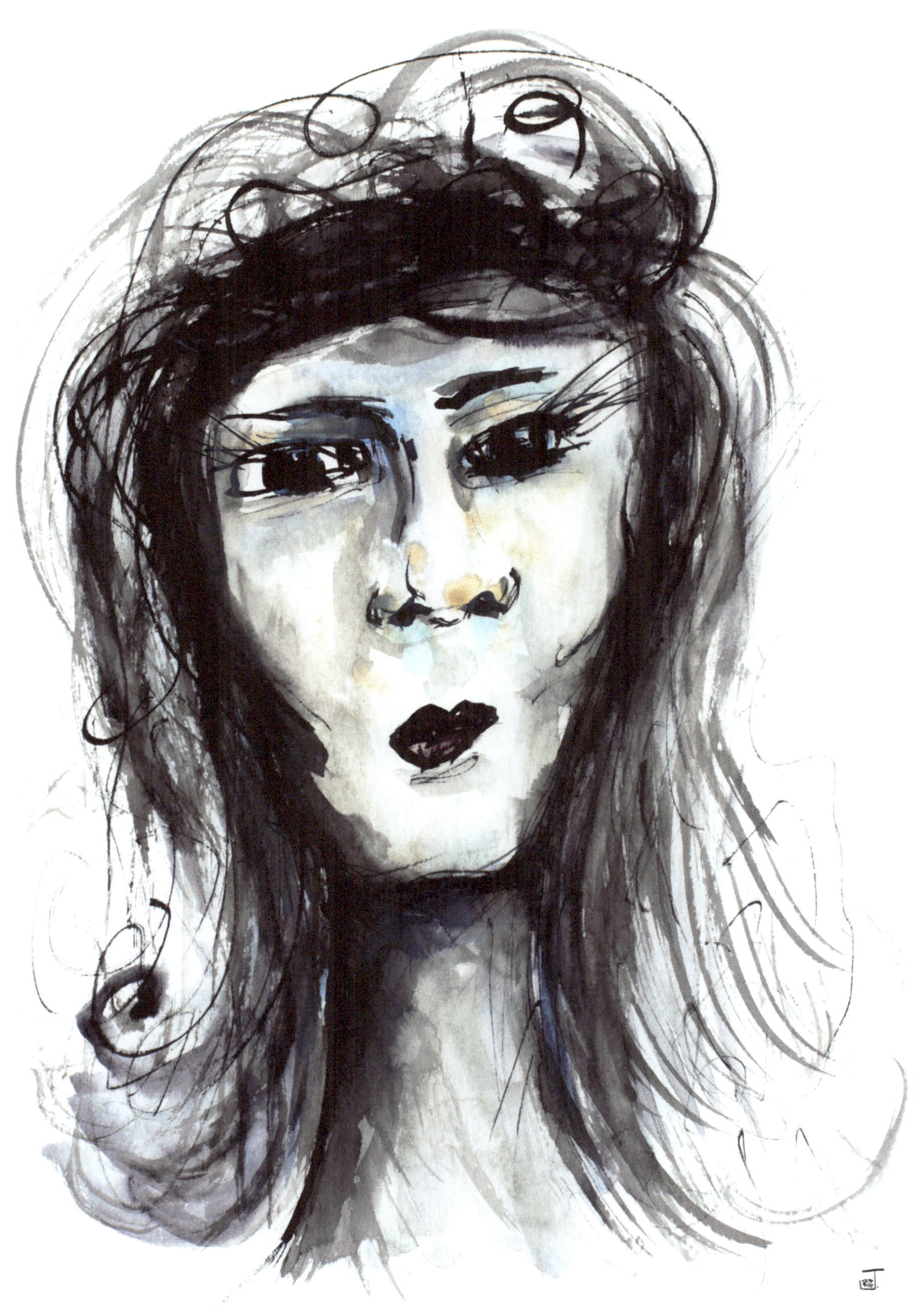

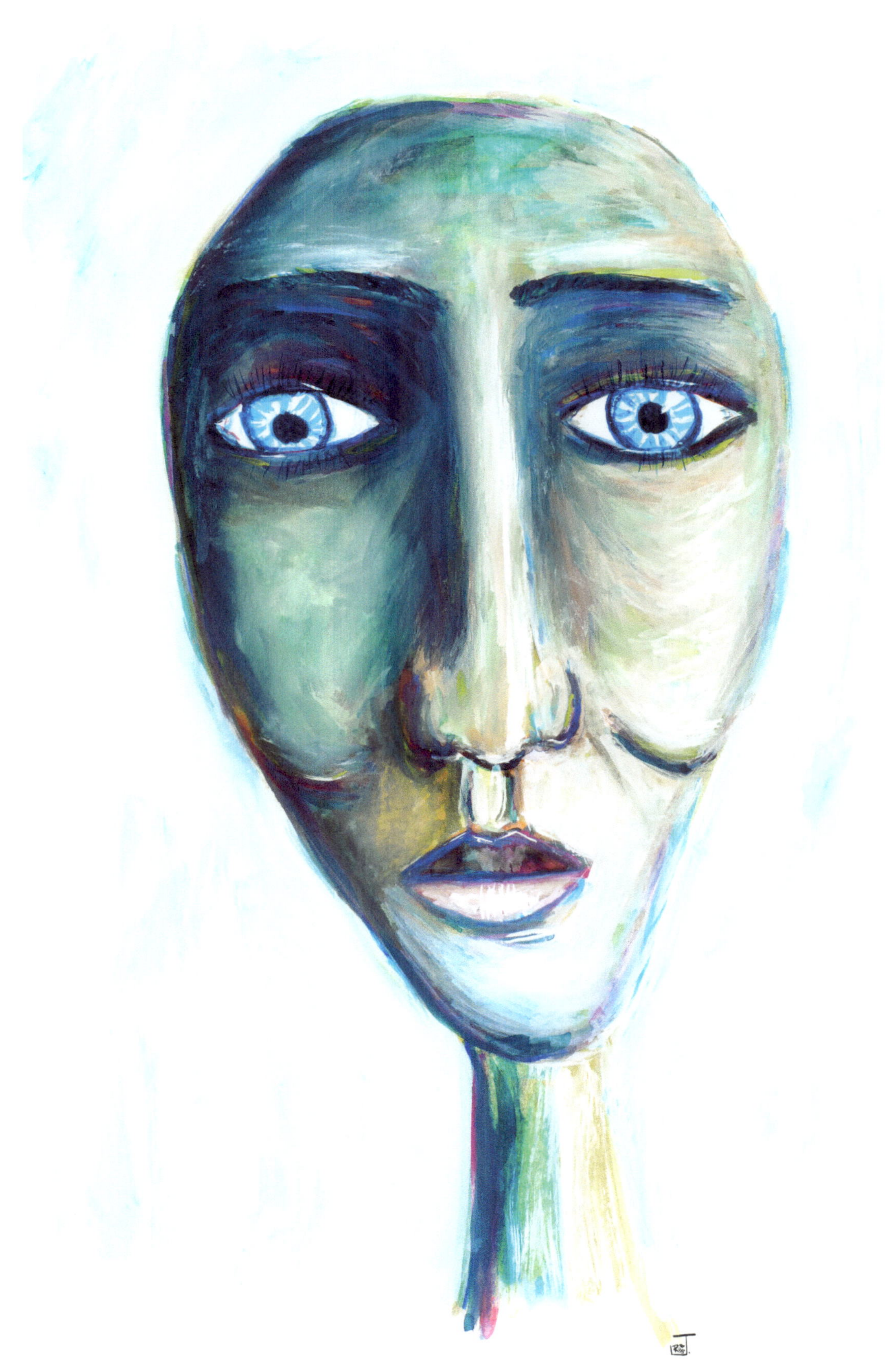

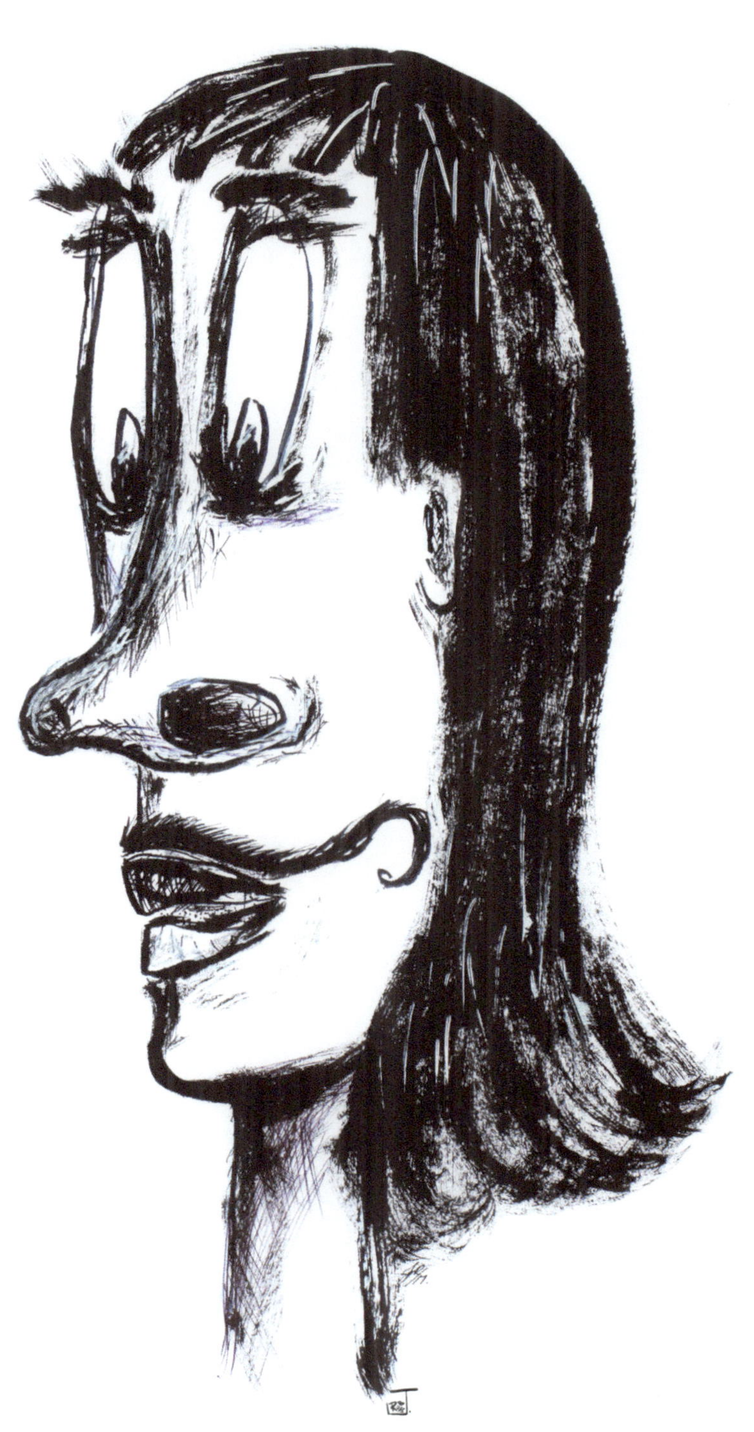

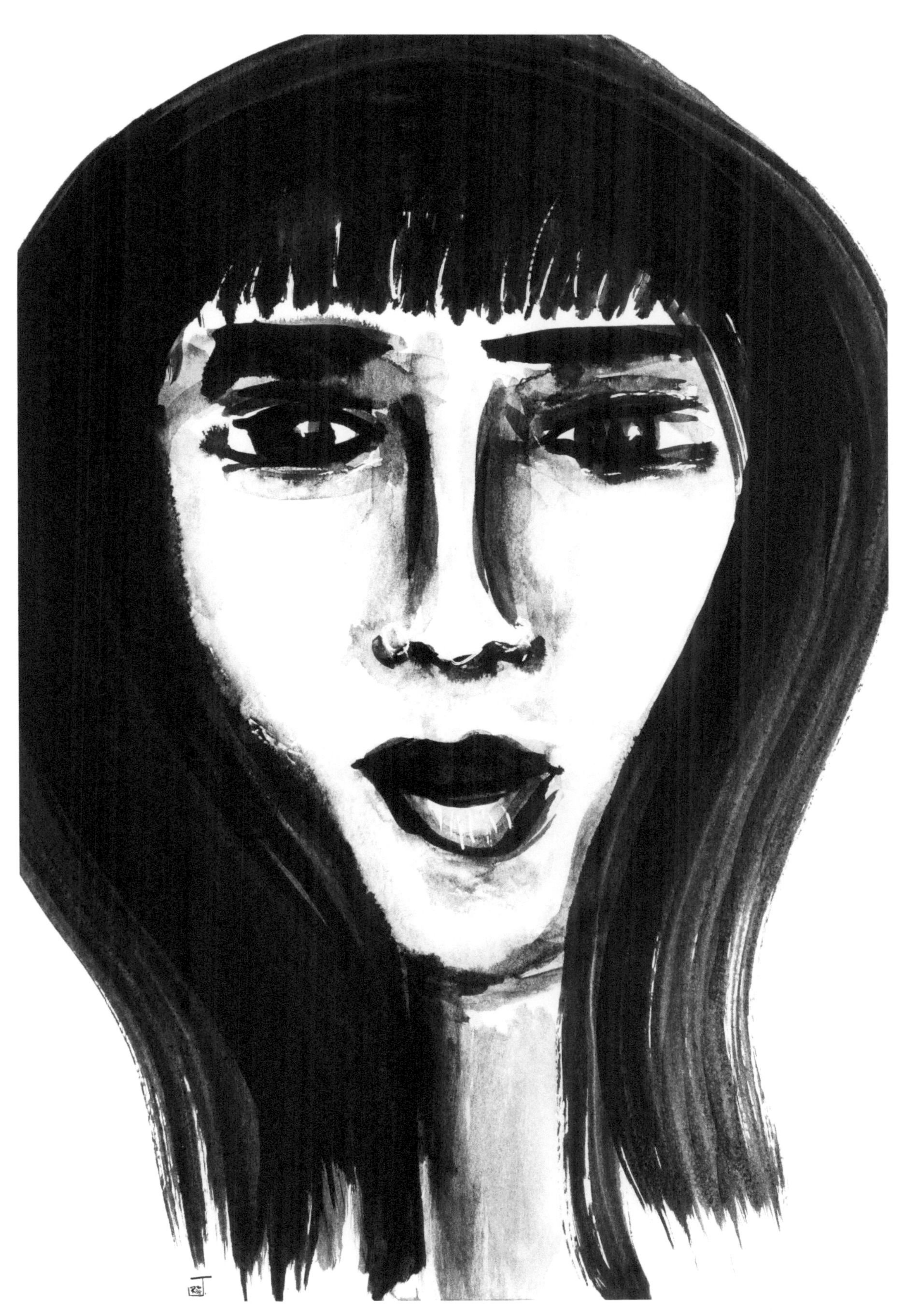

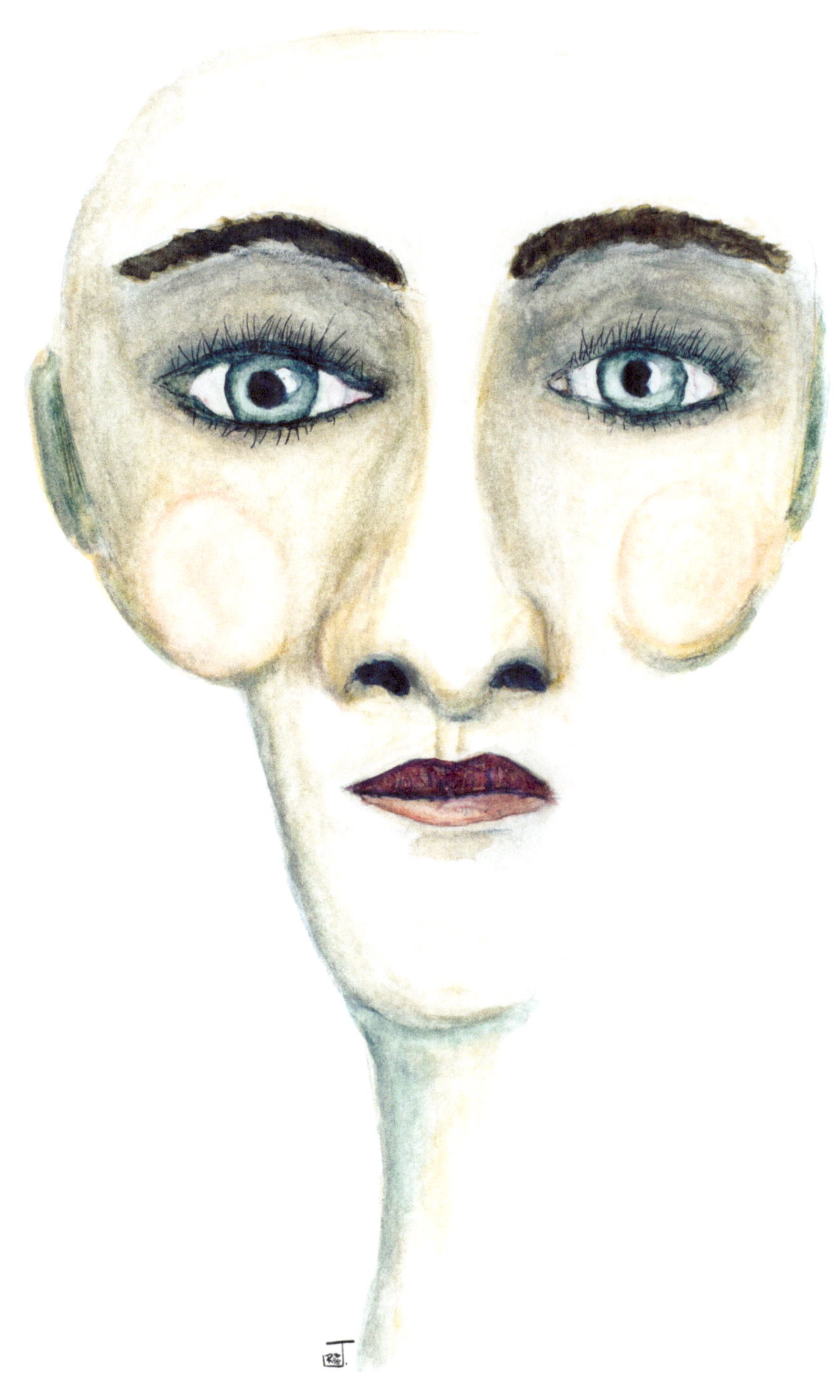

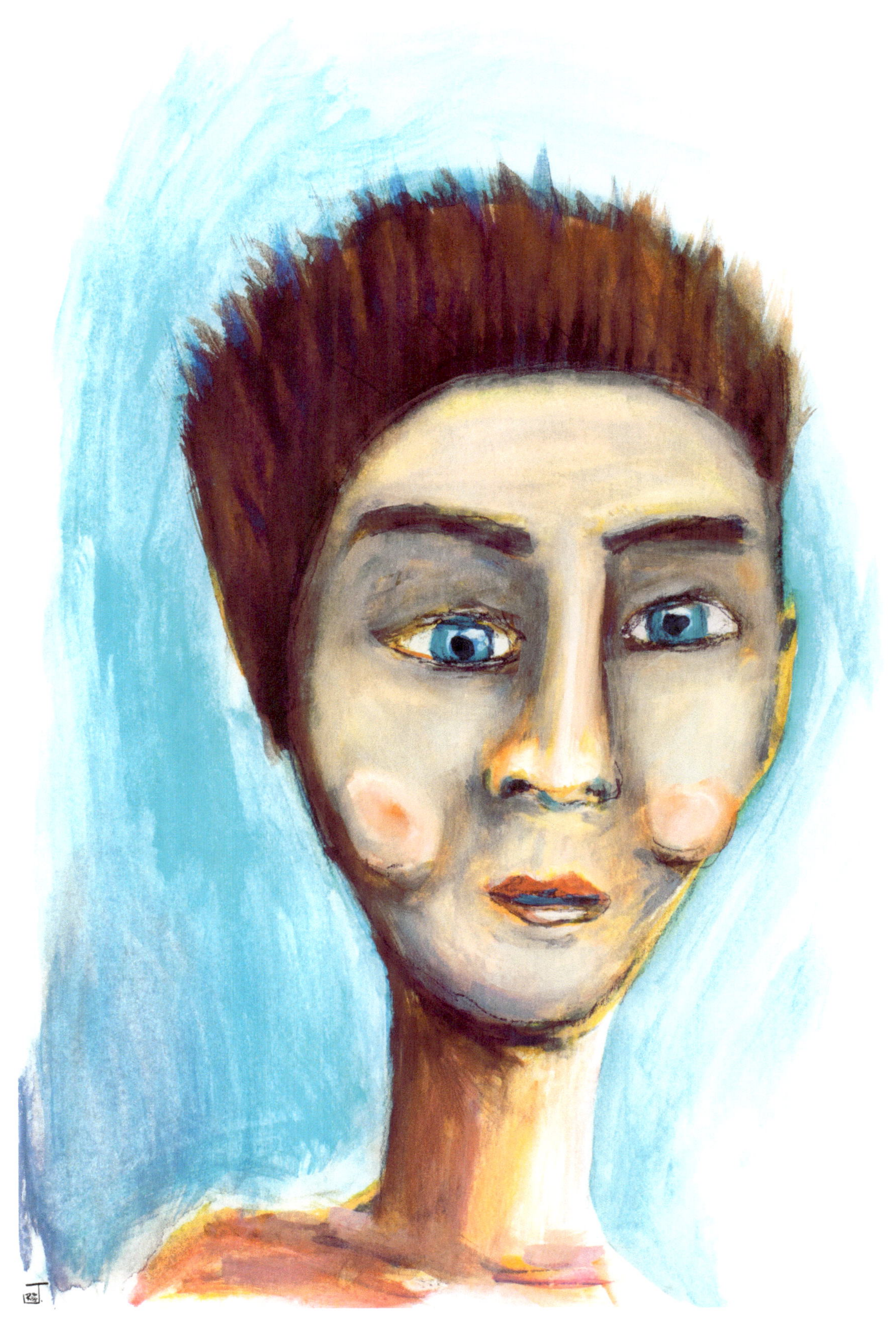

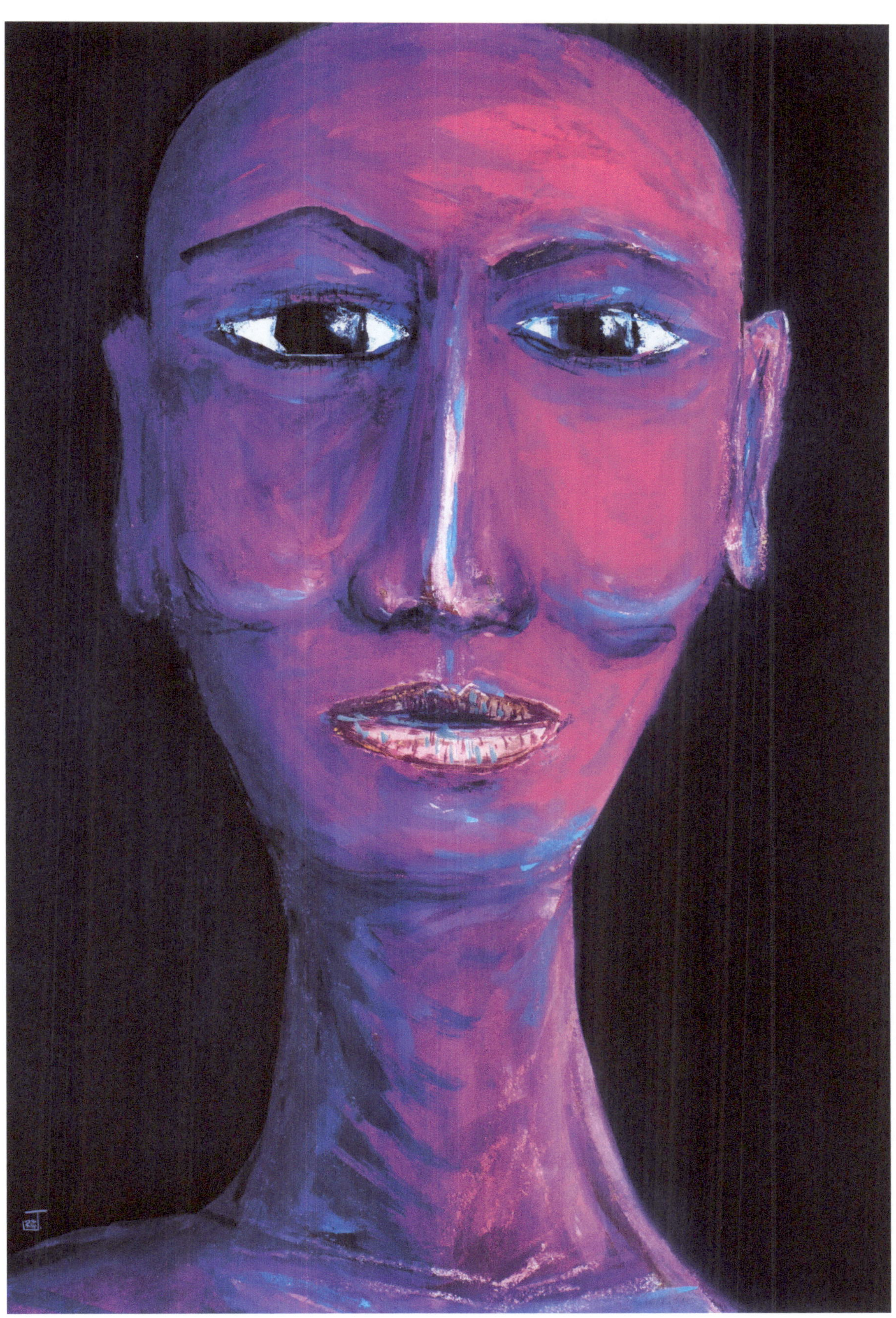

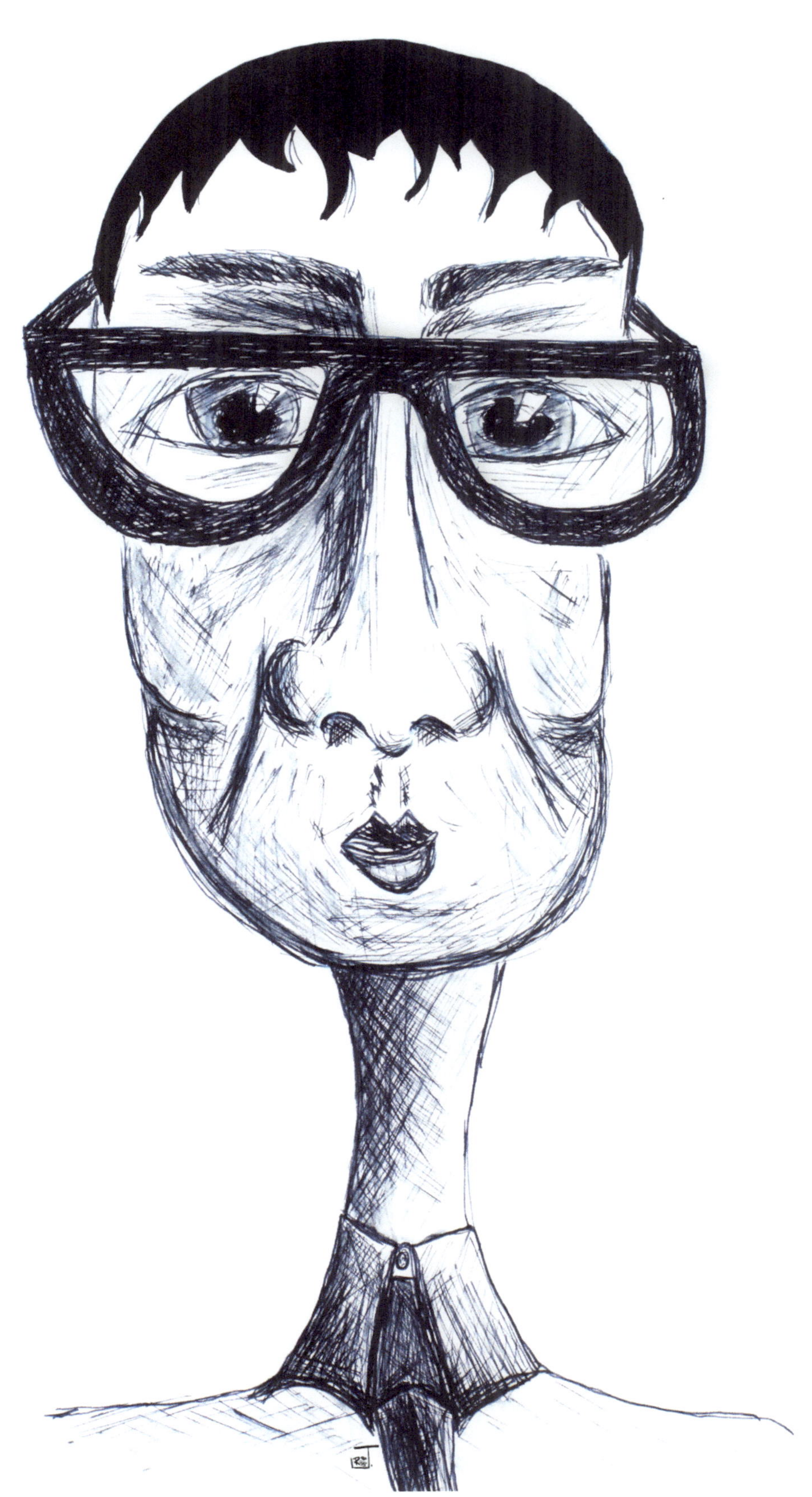

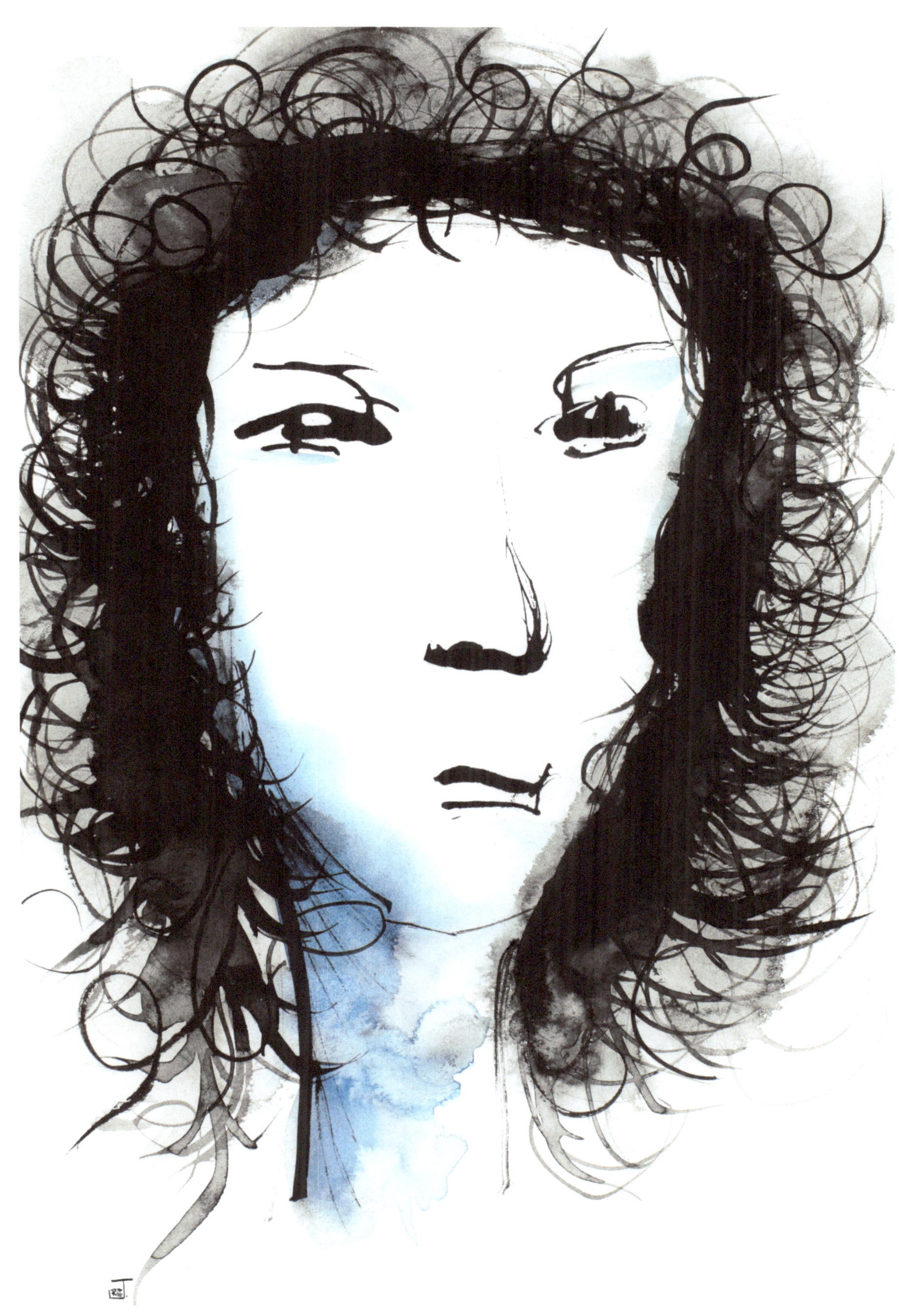

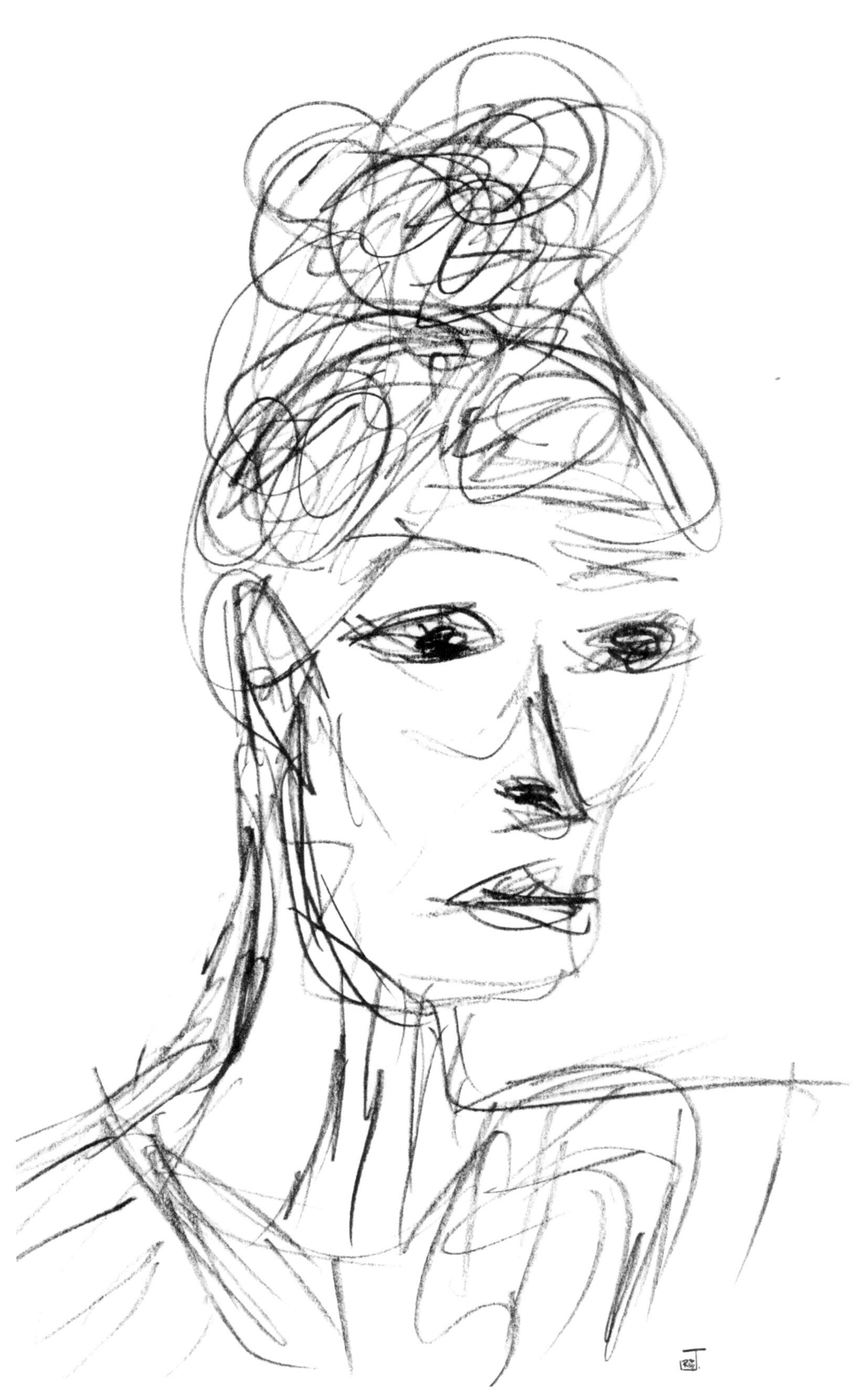

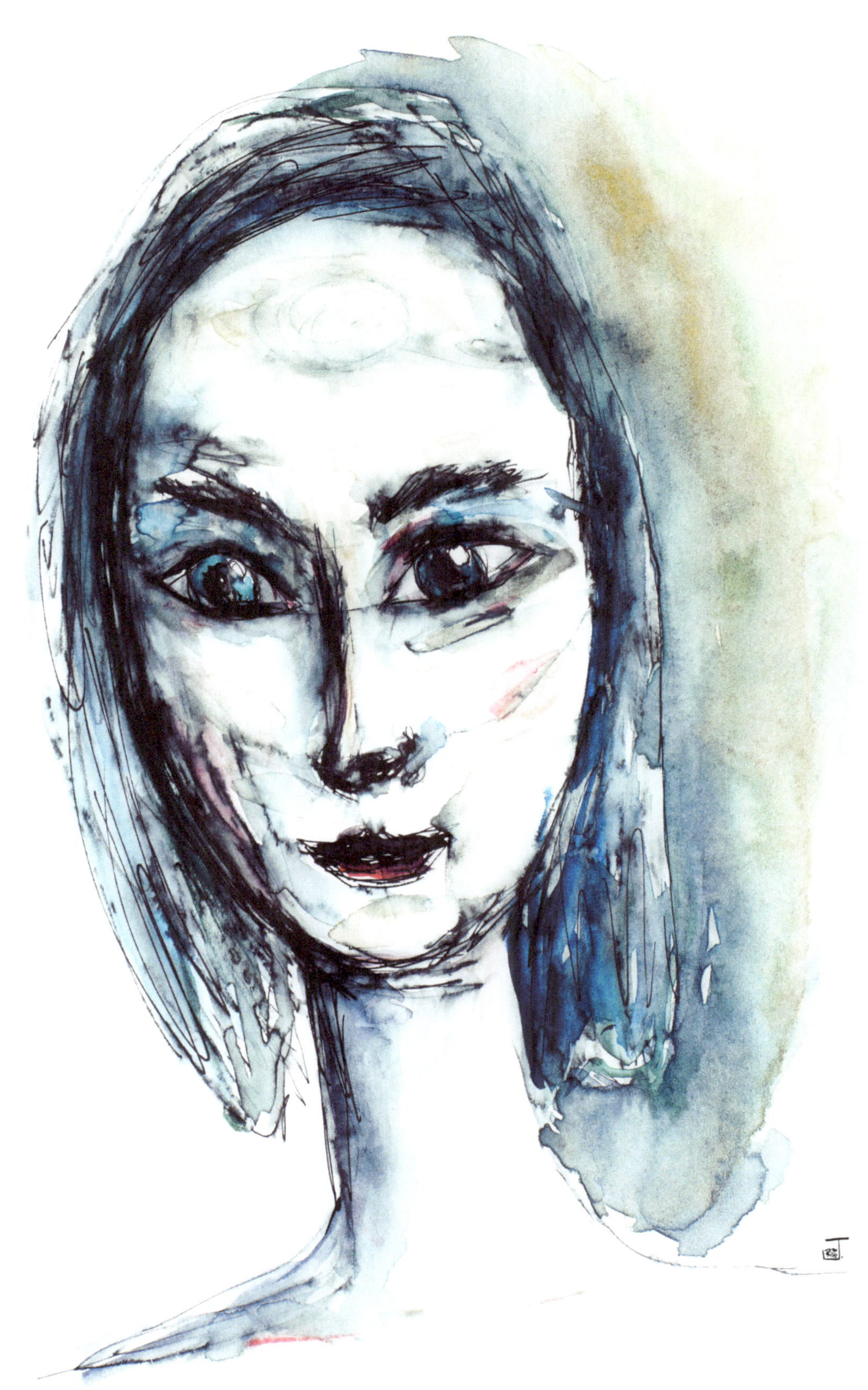

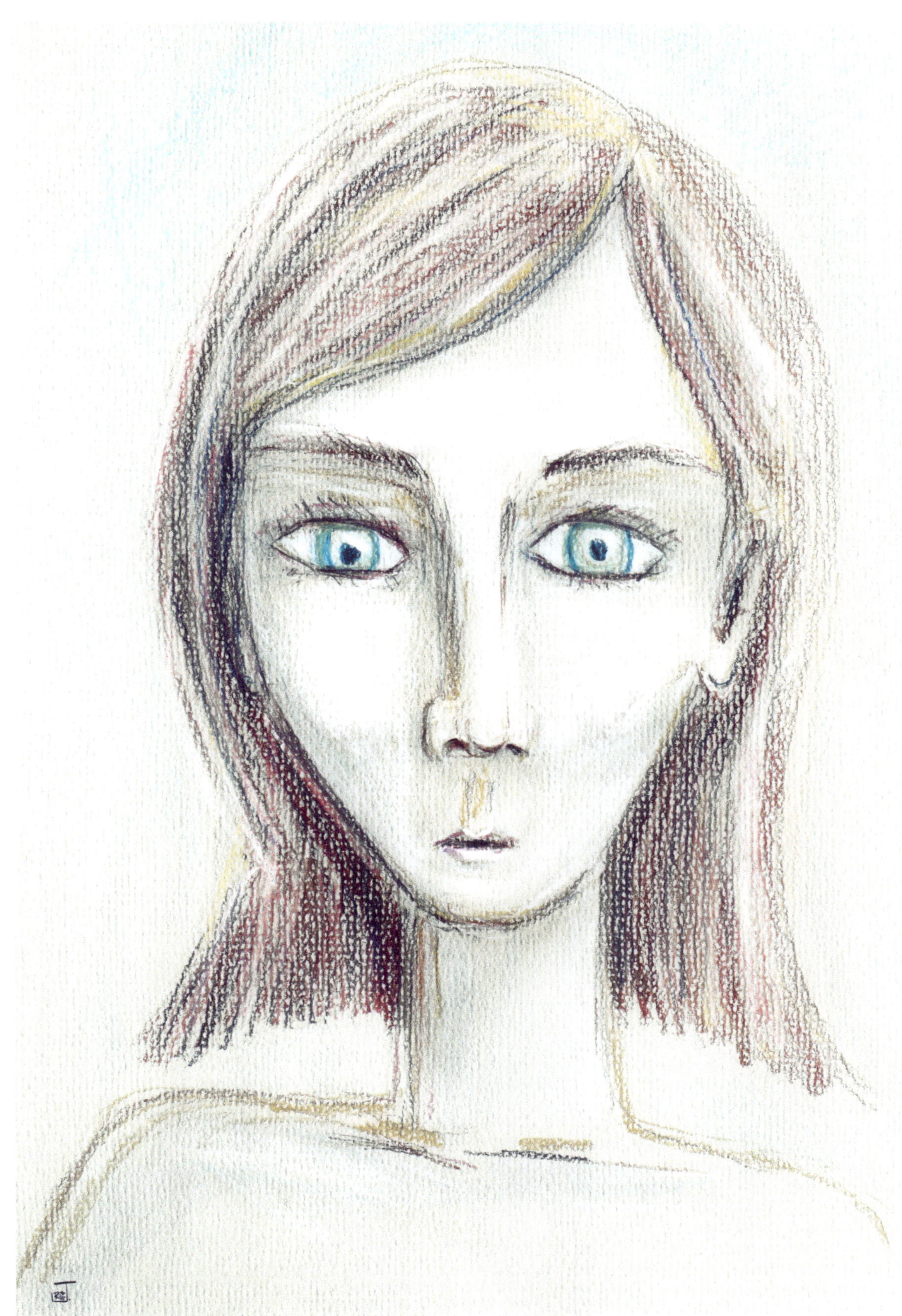

50 Faces; illustrated portrait art
Published by NoooBooks, 2020
Tweed Heads, NSW, Australia.
Copyright: © NoooBooks

Imagery is a blend of traditional techniques, ink, watercolour, gouache, oil pastel, soft pastel illustrations.

The paper this book is printed on is FSC® certified (Forest Stewardship Council®).
FSC promotes environmentally responsible, socially beneficial and
economically viable management of the world's forests.

A catalogue record for this book is available
from the National Library of Australia.
ISBN: 978-1-922415-04-2

More NoooBooks...

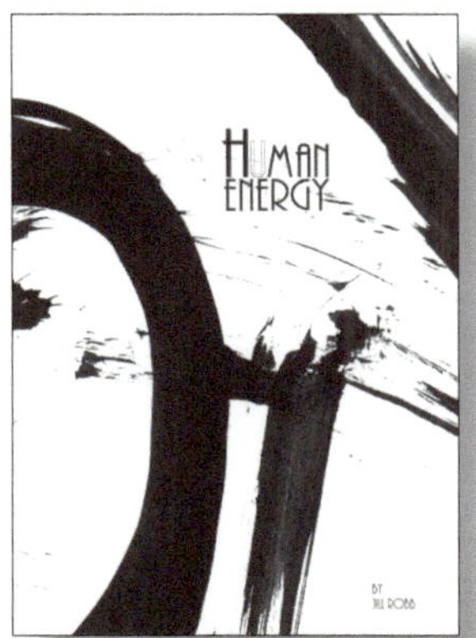

Human Energy
A Sumi-E Art Story,
Jill Robb
ISBN: 978-1-925991-41-3

An abstract figurative inky Picture book
for adults exploring human energies,
such as love, life and dance.

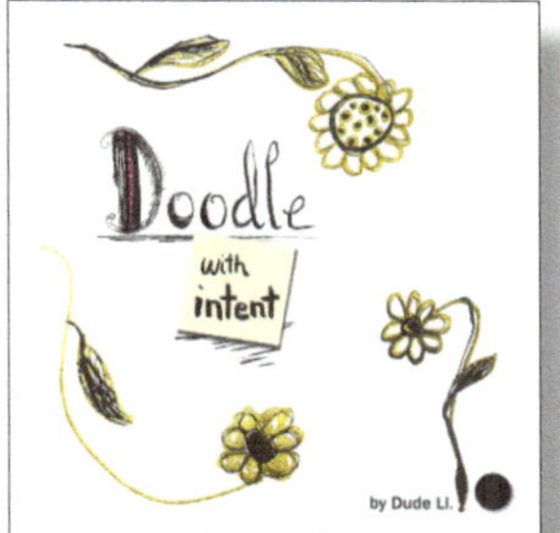
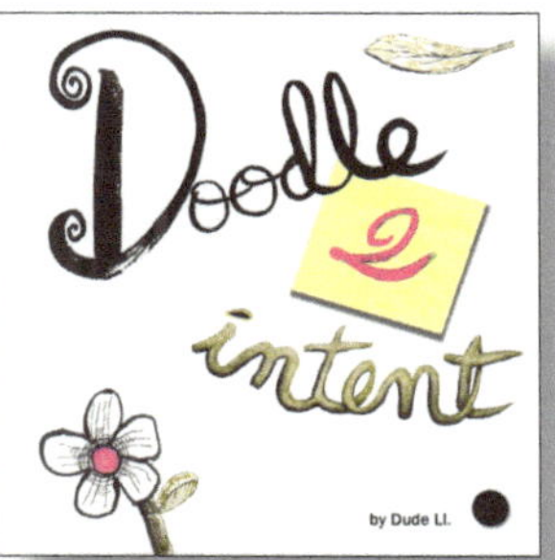

Doodle with Intent (series)
Dude Ll.
Book 1 ISBN:978-1-925991-50-5
Book 2 ISBN:978-1-925991-81-9

Nonsensical illustrated adult picture books about
the quirky good in life.

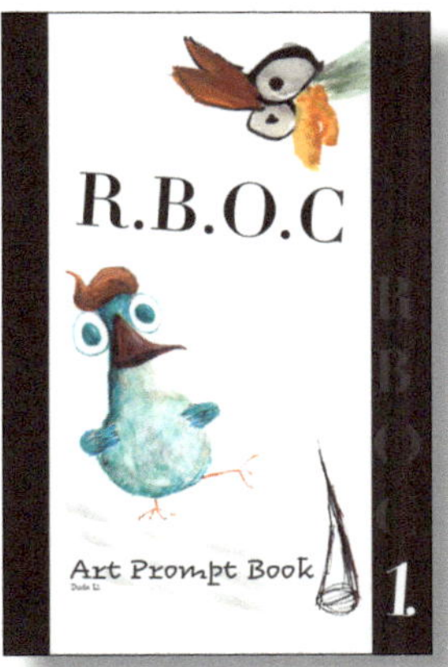
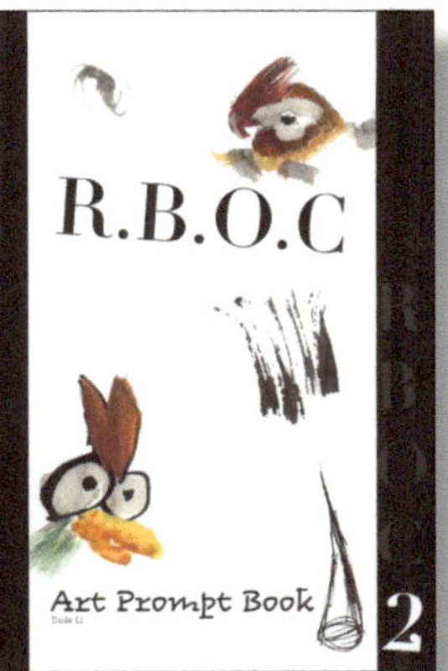
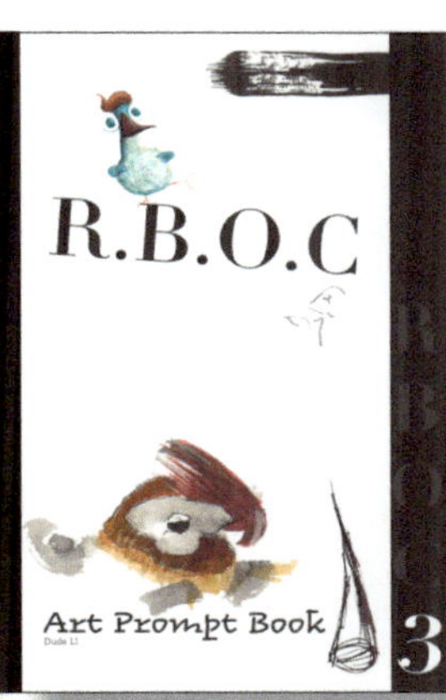

R.B.O.C (series)
Dude Ll.
Book 1 ISBN: 978-1-925991-43-7
Book 2 ISBN: 978-1-925991-44-4
Book 3 ISBN: 978-1-925991-45-1

Art Prompt books with a range of visual cues of inky
marks and Random Bits Of Crap on the pages to
inspire your doodles. Convenient Hardcover size
perfect for commuting and travel.

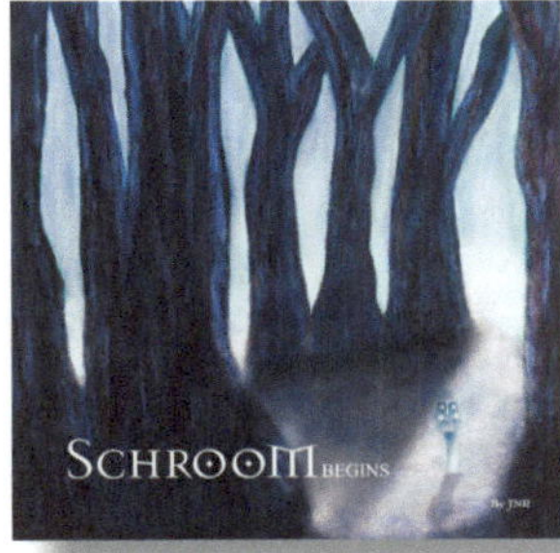

Schroom: begins
Picture book Ages 3-6
JNR
Book 1 ISBN: 978-1-925991-42-0

Schroom is a daydreamer,
a little mushroom always dreaming
of doing far-out things and going to
far-out places.
The story begins with Schroom in the
forest where he begins to dream. He
imagines fantastic things, until one day
he does something special.

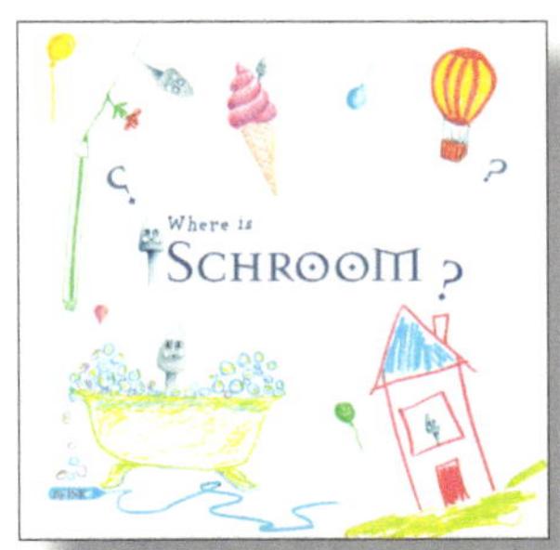

Where is Schroom?
Drawing Activity book
Ages 3-8
JNR
ISBN:978-1-925991-80-2

One to spark the imagination, Grab
your pencils and draw fun places around
Schroom. There are short prompts to
spark ideas in young minds, a book to
draw in their own fun, imaginative and
ideal places for Schroom to be…

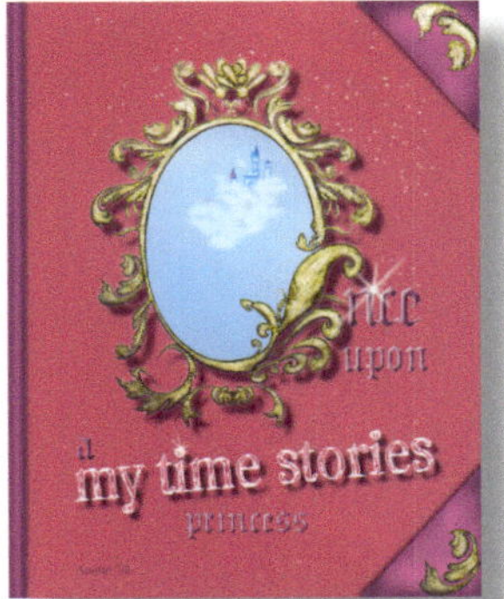
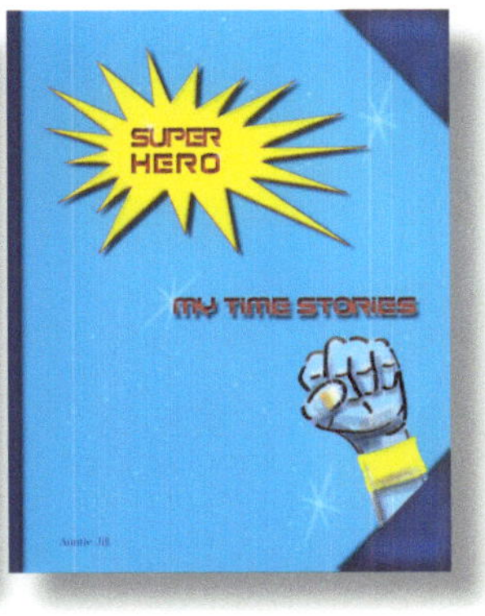

My Time Stories
Themed story writing books
Auntie Jill
'Once Upon a my time stories- Princess' ISBN: 978-1-925991-39-0
'My Time stories- Super Hero' ISBN:978-1-925991-71-0

Styled enchanted story writing books for your little Princess and Superhero
to tell their stories.
A page of writing tips, ruled lines and spaces for illustrations on these
beautiful colourful decorated pages.

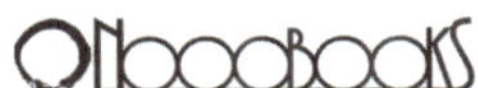